THE COST OF GRACE

JERRY OKOJIE

THE COST OF GRACE

JERRY OKOJIE

THE COST OF GRACE
©2017 Jerry Okojie

ISBN 978-1-64136-571-0

Christ The Solution Ministries

www.christthesolution.org
pastor@christthesolution.org
+353877505104

All rights reserved. No portion of this book may be
reproduced in
any form, except for brief quotations, without the written
permission
of the publishers.

All scripture quotations are from the New King James Version
(NKJV) and the
Amplified bible, except otherwise stated.

DEDICATION

To My Personal Lord and Saviour, Jesus Christ, who is the faithful witness, the first begotten of the dead, and the prince of the kings of the earth. Unto him that ever loved us and washed us from our sins in his own blood, And hath made us kings and priests unto God and His Father; to him be glory and dominion forever and ever. Amen.

TABLE OF CONTENTS

ACKNOWLEDGEMENT	ix
INTRODUCTION	1
CHAPTER ONE WHAT ABOUT GRACE?	3
CHAPTER TWO THE COST	29
CHAPTER THREE THE CAUSE	123
CHAPTER FOUR THE EFFECT	141
CHAPTER FIVE THE APPLICATION OF GRACE	171
CONCLUSION	211

ACKNOWLEDGEMENT

All the glory be to the Father, Son and Holy Spirit for making my life meaningful and beautiful. As for me and my household, we will serve you, dearest JESUS!

Special appreciation to every vessel: friends, siblings, family members, saints of God under my care, mentors who the Blessed Lord has used in any way to add value to my life. May the good Lord grant you all your heart's desires.

My sincere appreciation to my beloved and beautiful wife, Pastor Betty Okojie, for her unending support and encouragement; also for typing this book. May the Good Lord continue to keep you strong and young. Blessed are you among women. To our beloved children, you are all deeply loved and highly valued. May the Hand of the Lord continue to rest on you all in Jesus' Name.

INTRODUCTION

A few years back, I was asleep one night and had a dream; better put, it was really more of a vision of the night. I called it a vision of the night because there was no activity, but only a picture. I saw in that vision a book shelf, arranged with different books. It was as though my eyes were zoomed in to one book on the shelf. The particular book was titled: THE COST OF GRACE by Jerry Okojie. The colour of the book was green, with the words written in white. Then the vision came to an end. As I awoke from sleep, I understood straight away what it meant; obviously, to write a book according to the revealed titled. The same Lord who has graciously chosen and commissioned me to write this book has also generously downloaded the content into my Spirit-man. The outcome is this revelatory book in your hands.

Covered within the contents of this heavenly-sent book are interesting definitions of the word 'grace', with both familiar and fresh insight; extensive expose on what it cost God to make grace available and accessible to mankind; the motivating factor behind the benevolence acts of God; the effects of the gracious and sacrificial acts of God; and lastly, the application on the part of the recipients of grace.

As you read carefully through the pages of this book, may you see and comprehend why Heaven deemed it necessary for this book to be written and then apprehended me to write it. Read with grace in Jesus' name.

CHAPTER ONE
WHAT ABOUT GRACE?

"But Noah found grace in the eyes of the LORD."
- Genesis 6:8

Grace as a Word

The word '*grace*' appears in the Old Testament 38 times. The Hebrew word that translates to grace is '*chen*', pronounced '*khane*'. The same word is translated as '*favour*' 26 times; '*gracious*' two times; '*pleasant*' one time; and as '*precious*' one time. When the word is used subjectively, it means kindness or favour. But when it is used objectively, it denotes beauty. Therefore, grace simply means favour: what is pleasant and agreeable.

The first mention of the word grace in the New Testament is found in Luke 2:40. The Greek word translated to grace in the New Testament is '*charis*', pronounced as '*khar'-ece*'; it implies the divine influence upon the heart and its reflection in life. The same word is also translated as '*acceptable*'. Hence, grace means acceptance or acceptable in God's eyes. Grace indicates favour on the part of the giver, but thanks on the part of the receiver.

Grace is an attribute of God. It is manifested in God's tender sense of our misery, which displays itself in His efforts to lesson and entirely remove it. Such effort is sometimes hindered and defeated only by means of continued perverseness. God's grace removes guilt, and His mercy removes misery from all who trust and hope in Him.

Objectively, grace is that which bestows or occasions pleasure and delight, or that causes favourable regards. Subjectively, on the part of the bestowal, it is the friendly or parental disposition from which the kindly acts proceed. It entails graciousness, loving-kindness, and goodwill generally.

Grace is though favour, yet implies more than

favour. Grace is a free gift. Favour may be deserved, earned, or gained, but grace is unearned, underserved, unmerited, and cannot be gained. Grace is universally free, thus, set in contrast with dept (Romans 4:4,16); contrast with work (Romans 11:6); and contrast with law (John 1:17, Romans 6:14,15, Galatians 5:4.)

Grace is a favour one receives without any merit of his or her own. God is the only donor of grace that He freely bestowed upon sinners. Beyond unmerited favour, grace is God's endowments upon believers by the operation of the Holy Spirit in the Churches:

> *"Having then gifts differing according to the grace that is given to us, whether prophecy, let us prophesy according to the proportion of faith;"* Romans 12:6

> *"But unto every one of us is given grace according to the measure of the gift of Christ."* Ephesians 4:7

> *"As every man hath received the gift, even so*

minister the same one to another, as good stewards of the manifold grace of God." **1 Peter 4:10.**

Grace as God's Nature

"And the LORD passed by before him, and proclaimed, The LORD, The LORD God, merciful and gracious, longsuffering, and abundant in goodness and truth," **Exodus 34:6**

Grace is more than a word; it is God's nature. Our God, the maker of the heaven and the earth, is gracious. The Hebrew word translated to '*gracious*' in those verses is '*channuwn*', pronounced as '*khan-noon*'; this adjective in Hebrew is used only of God and denotes the action that springs from His free and unmerited love to His creatures. This is what is intend to dig out and highlight above all else as the true definition of grace. Grace is as the parental bond between a child and their parents, especially a motherly bond with her child. It is the kind of love that makes a man desire and decide to have a family of a wife and kids.

> *"And he said, I will make all my goodness pass before thee, and I will proclaim the name of the LORD before thee; and will be gracious to whom I will be gracious, and will shew mercy on whom I will shew mercy."*
> **Exodus 33:19**

God is gracious in acts. He is especially the only source of undeserved favour. This is why we ask Him repeatedly for such gracious acts as only He can offer (Numbers 6:25). The other Hebrew word translated as gracious is '*chanan*', pronounced '*khaw-nan*'; this word implies to bend or stoop in kindness to an inferior; to move to favour by petition; to be considerate. The word generally implies the extending of favour, often when it is neither expected nor deserved. It may also express generosity and a gift from the heart. God's favour is especially seen in His deliverance from one's enemies or surrounding evils. However, God extends His graciousness in His own sovereign way and wills that to whomever He chooses, as echoed in the verse above.

While in prayer on February 20th, 2017, the Sovereign Lord unveiled to me a fresh revelation of grace. I was made to understand that God's grace and graciousness is the omni-benevolence and sovereign acts of the Omnipotent, Omniscient, and Omnipresent Creator to make Himself available and accessible to His beloved creatures. Our God is truly gracious, particularly as the prime basis of His relationship with mankind, which has always been the instance and will forever be. Grace is therefore a contact point at which humanity has contact with divinity. It is the only parameter for God having a relationship and intimacy with humans. And likewise, it is the only parameter by which humans have true devotion and experiential worship with their maker: God.

> *"Wherefore we receiving a kingdom which cannot be moved, let us have grace, whereby*

WHAT ABOUT GRACE?

we may serve God acceptably with reverence and godly fear:" **Hebrews 12:28**

As evidential from that verse of scripture, it is only by grace that humans can serve God acceptably with reverence and godly fear. The Amplified version of the Bible renders that verse in a more interesting manner; it said to: *"...offer to God pleasing service and acceptable worship..."* rightly implying that the only acceptable way of offering to God pleasing service and reverential worship is through His grace. In a nutshell, grace is the parental bond between divinity and humanity. The empathy of a mother to her child is a reflection of God binding compassion with humans.

> *"But Zion said, The LORD hath forsaken me, and my Lord hath forgotten me. Can a woman forget her sucking child, that she should not have compassion on the son of her womb? yea, they may forget, yet will I not forget thee. Behold, I have graven thee upon the palms of my hands; thy walls are continually before me."* **Isaiah 49:14-16**

THE COST OF GRACE

> *"As one whom his mother comforteth, so will I comfort you; and ye shall be comforted in Jerusalem."* **Isaiah 66:13**

It obvious, in light of these two distinct verses of scripture, that grace is truly the paternal and maternal nature of the Almighty God. He affirms that even if a mother may forget her suckling child (as rare as that may seem), He will never forget us. Implying that His compassion for His children far surpasses that of a mother to her child. Also implied in that statement is His motherly nature or trait, which is His graciousness. On the other hand, Psalm 103:8-14 unveils to us God's paternal or fatherly nature.

> *"The LORD is merciful and gracious, slow to anger, and plenteous in mercy. He will not always chide: neither will he keep his anger for ever. He hath not dealt with us after our sins; nor rewarded us according to our iniquities. For as the heaven is high above the earth, so great is his mercy toward them that*

fear him. As far as the east is from the west, so far hath he removed our transgressions from us. Like as a father pitieth his children, so the LORD pitieth them that fear him. For he knoweth our frame; he remembereth that we are dust." **Psalm 103:8-14**

All the blessed characteristics exhibited in this passage are a vivid portrait of a loving and compassionate father's heart. In verse 13, the word says: as a father loves and pities his children, so the Lord pities us that fear Him. This gracious image of the Father was graphically painted to us by the Lord Jesus Christ in the parable of the prodigal son in Luke chapter 15.

In that familiar story, the son left home with most of the father's wealth; broke the father's heart and went to squander it all. But the father's action was completely equivalent to the text above. He stayed merciful and gracious toward his son. In His reaction, he was slow to anger and plenteous in mercy. We have no record of him chiding or contending with his son, neither did he keep his anger against Him. When the boy finally returned back home, the father did not deal with him after his sin nor did he reward him according to his iniquities.

To prove that he removed the boy's sins as far as the east is from the west, the father never said a word about his son doing wrong and didn't even want to hear him apologize for it. Rather, he had pity on him and changed his raiment, putting shoes on his feet and a ring on his hand as an affirmation of his extravagant love and graciousness. He even threw an extravagant homecoming party for him. Wow! What a perfect picture of our gracious heavenly Father. Although we, like sheep, had gone astray, every man to his own way, the Father laid on Christ the sin of us all. Men and brethren, this is an exhibition of grace and it is indeed amazing!

The Shadow of Grace

"For the law having a shadow of good things to come, and not the very image of the things,

can never with those sacrifices which they offered year by year continually make the comers thereunto perfect. For then would they not have ceased to be offered? because that the worshippers once purged should have had no more conscience of sins. But in those sacrifices there is a remembrance again made of sins every year. For it is not possible that the blood of bulls and of goats should take away sins. Wherefore when he cometh into the world, he saith, Sacrifice and offering thou wouldest not, but a body hast thou prepared me: In burnt offerings and sacrifices for sin thou hast had no pleasure. Then said I, Lo, I come (in the volume of the book it is written of me,) to do thy will, O God. Above when he said, Sacrifice and offering and burnt offerings and offering for sin thou wouldest not, neither hadst pleasure therein; which are offered by the law; Then said he, Lo, I come to do thy will, O God. He taketh away the first, that he may establish the second. By the which will

we are sanctified through the offering of the body of Jesus Christ once for all. And every priest standeth daily ministering and offering oftentimes the same sacrifices, which can never take away sins: But this man, after he had offered one sacrifice for sins for ever, sat down on the right hand of God; From henceforth expecting till his enemies be made his footstool. For by one offering he hath perfected for ever them that are sanctified."
Hebrew 10:1-14

As we have discussed earlier, the only basis or parameters at which divinity reveals Himself and relates intimately with humanity is absolutely and exclusively through the medium of grace. Grace is what brings us into relationship with God. Right from the beginning of creation, God's intimate relationship with Adam and Eve was based in grace. It was in grace that they were made habitations of the Holy Spirit. But when they sinned against God, they committed high treason, and as a result, they lost their home. More than that, they fell from grace and also lost the indwelling Holy Spirit in them. Consequently, Adam and Eve were not the only one who lost their home; God the Holy Spirit also lost His home in the process. It may be helpful for you to know that the garden where they lived was grace, namely Eden: meaning delight; which is a synonyms of grace. Hence, when they were kicked out of Eden, they were kicked out of grace.

Amazingly, when our first parents were out of the garden, they still had a good relationship with God. Nevertheless, it wasn't as near as it used to be. For in the absence of grace, they no longer enjoyed intimacy as they once did, but had a distant and external relationship. We all can definitely relate with that. Once a close trusted friend betrays us, even when the issue is resolved and has been reconciled, it can only take the special grace of God to enjoy the previous level of intimacy. As they say: once beaten, twice shy.

But after the fall, God, who is unlike man, put into motion His divine plan to restore mankind back to full intimacy with Himself. He made a promise in Genesis 3:15 in regards to the seed of the woman who will come and destroy the works of the devil and restore man back to the Eden of grace, as foreshadowing of the promised Messiah, who is to come as a Lamb to take away the sins of the world. God slew a literal lamb as a temporary atonement for their sins and clothed them with coat of skin, which was far better than their designer fig leaves. Under the Laws, sacrifices and temple worship were a shadow of the good things or grace to come, and the participants could not have a perfect relationship that God desires. The best these could do was to maintain and foster a distant covenant relationship with a holy God. In this state, God was not satisfied and men helplessly yearned to be closer with their God but could not help it. The missing link was GRACE; it had disappeared at the fall.

Someone may be wondering how I knew that. Well, obviously from the scriptures. In Genesis 6:8, the scripture said Noah found grace in the eyes of the

Lord. Likewise, in Exodus 33:13, Moses petitioned the Lord. His argument was "*if I have found grace in your sight*", in the month of two witnesses every word is established. It shows that their respective relationship with the Lord is based on the fact that they had found grace in His sight. My question is: why does the Bible continually use the word found in conjunction with grace? The only scriptural answer would be because grace was missing from the scene, and was no longer available to all but to only the few that the Lord chose to sovereignly reveal it to.

If that does not convince you, then let's look at further proof from the New Testament. John 1:17 says the Law was given by Moses but Grace and Truth came by Jesus Christ. Mind the word used here; '*Grace and Truth came*'. '*Came*' means to come, arrive, or appear, which implies it was not formally on the scene or available. Titus 2:11 confirms it much more, saying, '*The grace of God that bringeth salvation has appear to all men*'. To appear is to be made manifest, to be on the scene.

This implied that it had disappeared earlier but has now appeared through Christ Jesus.

My point is that the missing link was grace; the absence of grace meant no salvation, no intimacy, and no indwelling presence of Holy Spirit. While the presence of grace is salvation, we can rightly conclude that every effort of the Father from the fall of Adam to the birth, suffering, death, burial, resurrection, and ascension of Jesus Christ was to make grace available and accessible before all men. In order words, both the Law and all the required sacrifices were all school masters to bring us to grace. (See Galatians 3:24-29, Hebrew 7:18-19).

The Era of Grace

> *"Likewise reckon ye also yourselves to be dead indeed unto sin, but alive unto God through Jesus Christ our Lord. Let not sin therefore reign in your mortal body, that ye should obey it in the lusts thereof. Neither yield ye your members as instruments of*

> *unrighteousness unto sin: but yield yourselves unto God, as those that are alive from the dead, and your members as instruments of righteousness unto God. For sin shall not have dominion over you: for ye are not under the law, but under grace. What then? shall we sin, because we are not under the law, but under grace? God forbid."*
Romans 6:11-15

The scripture says in John chapter one, verse seventeen, that the Law was given by Moses but grace and truth came by Jesus Christ. This speaks of two different eras of dispensations and their respective mediators. Law and Grace are both means of having a relationship with God on distinct terms. Under the Law mediated by Moses that we generally refer to as the Old Covenant, God stated His requirement for having a relationship with Israel and whosoever wished to have a relationship with Him. But the requirement of the Law was too high to meet and consequence for not meeting the holy standard of the Law was too high to pay. Yahweh in

His infinite mercies introduced and tolerated a temporary measure of the innocent animal sacrifice as a covering for sin until the fullness of time:

> *"But when the fulness of the time was come, God sent forth his Son, made of a woman, made under the law, To redeem them that were under the law, that we might receive the adoption of sons. And because ye are sons, God hath sent forth the Spirit of his Son into your hearts, crying, Abba, Father. Wherefore thou art no more a servant, but a son; and if a son, then an heir of God through Christ."*
Galatians 4:4-7.

The Person of Grace

This is what the scripture means by grace and truth came by Jesus Christ. The coming of Christ was the ushering in of a new era of grace also known as the New Covenant where an intimate relationship with God is solely based on grace upon grace as echoed by John 1:17, which states *"And of His fullness have all we received, and grace for grace"*. Under the Old Testament, a relationship with God was based on keeping the Law blamelessly, while under the New Testament, a relationship with God is based on grace and faith. The Law could only produce a distant relationship, but grace restored a personal and intimate relationship with God. Hence, the era of grace is the fulfilment of acceptable time and the day of salvation promised in the Old Testament.

The Lord Jesus announced this era in His first recorded sermon at the synagogue in Luke 4:19 as part of His earthly mission: to preach the acceptable year of the Lord. The acceptable year of the Lord is the dispensation of grace where the grace of almighty God has been made available and accessible to men through faith in the person and redemptive work of our Lord and Saviour Jesus Christ. Titus 2:11 drives the point home: *"For the grace of God that bringeth salvation has appeared to all men"*. Friends and brethren, this is where we are; not under the Law but under Grace. In other words, we live in the state of God's unmerited favour and spiritual blessings.

> *"LABORING TOGETHER [as God's fellow workers] with Him then, we beg of you not to receive the grace of God in vain [that merciful kindness by which God exerts His holy influence on souls and turns them to Christ, keeping and strengthening them–do not receive it to no purpose]. For He says, In the time of favor (of an assured welcome) I have listened to and heeded your call, and I have helped you on the day of deliverance (the day of salvation). Behold, now is truly the time for a gracious welcome and acceptance [of you from God]; behold, now is the day of salvation!"* 2 Corinthians 6:1-2 Amplified.

Grace as Divine Endowment

"And lest I should be exalted above measure through the abundance of the revelations, there was given to me a thorn in the flesh, the

messenger of Satan to buffet me, lest I should be exalted above measure. For this thing I besought the Lord thrice, that it might depart from me. And he said unto me, My grace is sufficient for thee: for my strength is made perfect in weakness. Most gladly therefore will I rather glory in my infirmities, that the power of Christ may rest upon me. Therefore I take pleasure in infirmities, in reproaches, in necessities, in persecutions, in distresses for Christ's sake: for when I am weak, then am I strong. I am become a fool in glorying; ye have compelled me: for I ought to have been commended of you: for in nothing am I behind the very chiefest apostles, though I be nothing. Truly the signs of an apostle were wrought among you in all patience, in signs, and wonders, and mighty deeds." **2 Corinthians 12:7-12**

Beyond the faultless truth that grace is unmerited favour, it is also a divine enablement. It's a supernatural blessing; it's a supernatural ability for a supernatural assignment. It's defined by the amplified version of the Bible in 2 Corinthians 6:1 as: "...*That merciful kindness by which God exerts His holy influence on souls and turns them to Christ, keeping and strengthening them...*" In other words, grace is God's divine endowment in our lives to influence us and enable us carry out His will on the earth.

In the text above, Apostle Paul unveils to us a fresh insight on what God and he personally sees grace to be. He stated that, because of the abundance of revelation God had privileged him with, there was given to him a messenger of Satan to buffet him. As much as I want to avoid the theological debate on who sent the evil messenger to buffet Paul, it suffice to say that God may have allowed it but did not send it; that being, it wasn't God's messenger but Satan's. The very fact that it was Satan's messenger shows who sent him. God has His own messengers and does not send Satan's messengers on missions against His will. As this messenger of hell continues to harass Paul, he must have rebuked it to no avail, and then he decided to seek the Lord's face specifically about the issue and that he did thrice.

I am curious why Paul would decide to keep the record and include it in his writing to us – how many times he besought the Lord over this issue. Could it be that he had not prayed over his personal issue that much or that he was overwhelmed and felt it was too much to handle? I am convinced that Paul as a man of faith and power of the Spirit was surprised at first, until the Lord used the situation to teach both him and us that there are certain mountains that God removes at our faith and prayers. But, there are other mountains that do not move at our cry, faith, or prayers; nonetheless, God gives us the grace to climb over them.

Paul's request was: *'Lord! Let this thing depart from me'*. God's response was: *'my grace is sufficient for thee: for my strength is made perfect in weakness'*. Within this statement is God's definition of what His grace is. He equates His grace with His Strength. Grace, therefore, is His strength made perfect in our weaknesses. Further proof of this is Apostle Paul's immediate reaction to God's response to his request. He declared: *'most gladly therefore will I glory in my infirmities, that the power of Christ May rest upon me'*.

"Power of Christ?" Who said anything so far about the power of Christ? Where did that ideal originate from? I am so glad you asked. It definitely came from Paul's understanding and interpretation of what God had said: that His strength is made perfect in weakness. He understood God's strength to be His grace, and interpreted it as the power of Christ.

In a nutshell, grace is Christ's divine ability or endowment for living and doing His will. This grace is not for the few but for every member of the Body of Christ. Each one of us has received grace in various capacities and also have an excess of grace available and accessible to us all.

> *"But unto every one of us is given grace according to the measure of the gift of Christ."*
> **Ephesians 4:7**

WHAT ABOUT GRACE?

"Having then gifts differing according to the grace that is given to us, whether prophecy, let us prophesy according to the proportion of faith;" **Romans 12:6**

CHAPTER TWO
THE COST

"Take heed therefore unto yourselves, and to all the flock, over the which the Holy Ghost hath made you overseers, to feed the church of God, which he hath purchased with his own blood."
Acts 20:28

Cost in business terms is an amount or price that has to be paid or given up in order to get something. It is usually a monetary valuation of effort, material, resources, time and utilities consumed, risks incurred, and opportunities forgone in the production and delivery of a good or service.

Due to the high cost of living, caused or

necessitated by global inflation from the recent economic meltdowns, most of us are burdened down daily with opportunity cost; what to acquire and what to forgo.

Often times, it all comes down to value and usefulness: *'Do I really need it or just want it?'* Sometimes it is not really a matter of 'if I need it or just want it' but truly a matter of if I can conveniently afford it. I drove passed a shop recently and saw through the window a very nice looking T-shirt that I liked. I immediately thought to myself, *'I don't think I can afford that now; beside, I have T-shirts at home to wear.'* What kept me from purchasing the shirt was the cost. I was not willing to pay the required price for it. To me, it wasn't worth it.

Unlike me in regards to the T-shirt, the price for our redemption was too high and costly to pay, but for God, it was worth it. The cost of a thing is usually associated with its worth or value. Value is the regard that something is held to determine its importance and usefulness. This leaves us with a trillion pound question: what is the value of a soul?

THE COST

The Value of a Soul

Unless we at least have an idea of its cost, we cannot in anyway understand the price paid to redeem it. Obviously, only the manufacturer knows the true cost of its product and has priced it accordingly in other to make a profit. In the same vein, only the Lord God, who created a soul, knows its value and cost. The customers are left with the choice of deciding if the product is worth the manufacturer's price to them or not. God not only knows the value of a soul as the creator but also as a customer who, in His unfailing mercies, had to purchase us back to Himself again. In Mark 8:36-37, the Lord gave us a clue of the cost, worth, or value of a soul.

> *"For what shall it profit a man, if he shall gain the whole world, and lose his own soul? Or what shall a man give in exchange for his soul?"*

In these two significant verses, the Lord is emphatically saying that all the world's goods and earthly treasures are not sufficient or equal to the worth of a soul. In other words, there is nothing one can give as a compensation or ransom in exchange for their soul. The soul or life of a man is priceless as far as earthly treasures are concerned. Of course, it has to be so, due to the fact that all things where created by God for the benefit of man. Man is the crown of creation, and as a result, nothing in all creation is more valuable than man. Which is why when mankind fell, creation also fell with them.

One other reason why the soul or life of a man is priceless is because: it is not of earthly origin. It is immortal and came out of the very breath of God Himself. According to Genesis 2:7, God formed man out of the dust of the earth, as He breathed unto his nostrils the breath of life; forthwith man became a living soul. When Adam and Eve sinned against God by eating the forbidden tree of knowledge of good and evil, although their soul became corrupted by that act, their worth and value to God remained the same. Hence, God was willing to pay the ultimate cost for His falling mankind.

THE COST

> *"For by grace are ye saved through faith; and that not of yourselves: it is the gift of God:"* **Ephesians 2:8**

As discussed earlier, before the fall, Adam was living in grace and had an intimate relationship with God through grace. After the fall, he was out of grace and fell from grace. The disobedience of Adam and Eve meant a rejection of the authority or leadership of the Lord God, which equals a fallen from grace. Apostle Paul in the New Testament warned the saints at Galatians of this:

> *"Stand fast therefore in the liberty wherewith Christ hath made us free, and be not entangled again with the yoke of bondage. Behold, I Paul say unto you, that if ye be circumcised, Christ shall profit you nothing. For I testify again to every man that is circumcised, that he is a debtor to do the whole law. Christ is become of no effect unto you, whosoever of you are justified by the*

> *law; ye are fallen from grace. For we through the Spirit wait for the hope of righteousness by faith."* **Galatians 5:1-5**

The warning here is that if they ever try to circumcise as a means of having right-standing with God, they would fall from grace as Adam and Eve did. My point is that, in Adam, mankind fell from grace and needed to be restored back to grace to have a right-standing with God again. There was no other way to go about it; man in his falling state had become helpless to help himself. It was all left for their loving Creator to devise a means to help man or else man would be doomed forever. The cry of Apostle Paul in Romans 7:24 captured the exact picture of our state of pity without grace:

> *"O wretched man that I am! who shall deliver me from the body of this death?"* **Romans 7:24**

The state of every man without the efficacious grace of Christ is nothing but wretchedness. But thank God through Jesus Christ we have received an abundance of grace and the gift of righteousness. Hence, what was required to restore man back to intimate relationship was not just forgiveness of sin but grace. It was saving grace that was needed, for it is grace alone that brings salvation. The price that was paid was to make the grace of God which brings salvation to appear before all men. It is by grace ONLY that men can be saved through faith.

The Incalculable Expense

> *"For God so loved the world, that he gave his only begotten Son, that whosoever believeth in him should not perish, but have everlasting life."* **John 3:16**

To truly appreciate the grace of God, one must understand the fall of man from grace and what it cost God to make grace available and accessible to all. In analysing the cost of grace, I would like to refer back to our business definition of how cost is measured. It is usually a monetary value of effort, material, resources, time and utility consumed, risk incurred, and opportunities forgone in the production and delivery of goods or services. Since we are not dealing with monetary issue, I would like to take that out of it and replace it with divine effort, making it contextual to the concept of this book.

In this context, cost is measured by divine value of effort, material resources, time and utility consumed, risk incurred, and opportunities foregone in the production and delivery of goods and services. In attempting to calculate in this chapter the incalculable expenses of grace, my intention is to use these business terms to vividly underscore the divine effort the Father made to make grace available. All divine material, all divine resources, all divine time and utility consumed, all divine risk incurred, and all divine opportunities forgone to bring salvation to humanity.

Heaven's Effort

"But Jesus answered them, My Father

THE COST

worketh hitherto, and I work." **John 5:17**

From the mouth of the master Himself, He said the Father has been working until now. He has never ceased working; He is still working and He too must be at divine work. What work is it that the Father has been doing until now and is still doing? Obviously, it's the work of grace in accordance with the good pleasure of His will which He has purposed in Himself before the foundation of the world. Most of us do not realize this; that God has worked effortlessly since the fall to restore man back to right-standing with Himself through grace. His effort includes trying all His best to preserve a linage through whom the promised seed of grace would come. This He did in the face of fiercest opposition from Satan and the rebellious will of man.

The greatest of all opposition to the divine agenda is not Satan directly but the stubborn will of mankind who are influenced by the devil. The will of man is the most powerful force on the face of the earth.

Why, you may ask? It is simply because God ordained it to be so. It was the edge mankind had over Satan and the angels. It is part of the God-likeness in us, meant to be an asset to replenish and subdue the earth on behalf of God. But Satan, through the fall, hijacked it and has since been using it against the plans and purposes of God. But against all odds, God successfully carried out His plan. He outsmarts the devil with His infinite wisdom.

The scripture said in 1 Corinthians 2:8: 'If the princes of this world had known, they would not have crucified the Lord of glory to their demise.' To make grace available and accessible, God had to find means to put down the rebellion of man without extinguishing mankind. In the case of Nimrod and the Tower of Babel, He had to confuse their language for them to abandon their defiance against His command to spread over the earth. In the case of righteous Noah, God had to destroy the then world for their violence and promiscuity to start afresh with Noah.

For the same reason, He called Abraham, Isaac, and Jacob through whom He birthed the nation of Israel, as His peculiar People and a chosen nation. He called Moses, and used him to deliver His people from the Egyptian bondage and brought them out to the Promised Land. Through Moses, God gave them a law, introduced priesthood and sacrifices. He raised up all kinds of minor and major prophets. He sets up and puts down mighty kings and nations. All these things God worked tirelessly into effect until the fullness of time came and a virgin conceived and gave birth to the Person of Grace and Truth.

Heavenly Material – His Body

"I am the living bread which came down from heaven: if any man eat of this bread, he shall live for ever: and the bread that I will give is my flesh, which I will give for the life of the world." **John 6:51**

"And as they were eating, Jesus took

bread, and blessed it, and brake it, and gave it to the disciples, and said, Take, eat; this is my body. And he took the cup, and gave thanks, and gave it to them, saying, Drink ye all of it; For this is my blood of the new testament, which is shed for many for the remission of sins." **Matthew 26:26-28**

The Lord's word that He is the bread from heaven signifies that the material required for our salvation by grace supersede earthly ones, 'for there is no name under heaven given among men whereby we must be saved'. As a result, God had to export from heaven a heavenly flesh. He said *"...and the bread that I will give is my flesh which I give for the life of the world."* This is what the bread in the communion signifies; for He said the bread is His body broken for us. What value can we place in the sinless body of Emmanuel? The scripture made us to understand in Hebrew chapter ten that because God was not pleased with the earth sacrifices that lacked the potential to make men perfect; he decided to prepare Him a body of heavenly origin. It was the offering of the body of Jesus Christ that sanctified and perfected us forever. It cost God the offering of the Body of His son to make grace available to humanity again.

> *"For it is not possible that the blood of bulls and of goats should take away sins. Wherefore when he cometh into the world, he saith, Sacrifice and offering thou wouldest not, but a body hast thou prepared me: In burnt offerings and sacrifices for sin thou hast had no pleasure. Then said I, Lo, I come (in the volume of the book it is written of me,) to do thy will, O God. Above when he said, Sacrifice and offering and burnt offerings and offering for sin thou wouldest not, neither hadst pleasure therein; which are offered by the law; Then said he, Lo, I come to do thy will, O God. He taketh away the first, that he may establish the second. By the*

which will we are sanctified through the offering of the body of Jesus Christ once for all. And every priest standeth daily ministering and offering oftentimes the same sacrifices, which can never take away sins: But this man, after he had offered one sacrifice for sins for ever, sat down on the right hand of God; From henceforth expecting till his enemies be made his footstool. For by one offering he hath perfected for ever them that are sanctified." **Hebrew 10:4-14**

Heavenly Resources – His Blood

"The next day John seeth Jesus coming unto him, and saith, Behold the Lamb of God, which taketh away the sin of the world." **John 1:29**

"In whom we have redemption through his blood, the forgiveness of sins,

according to the riches of his grace;"
Ephesians 1:7

The Lamb of God? What does John the Baptist mean by the Lamb of God? I am persuaded that what the greatest of all prophets was implying is: Here is all the heavenly resources enveloped in a bodily form as a sacrificial lamb. Ordained by God for the Passover of all mankind from death to life; grass to grace; darkness to light; poverty to prosperity; fear to faith; sickness to health; sin to righteousness; shame to glory; and from hell to heaven. (By the way, this is what made him the greatest of all the prophets as testified by the Lord Jesus: he is the only prophet that proclaimed Christ, actually saw Him in the flesh, endorsed and baptized Him).

> *"For there is one God, and one mediator between God and men, the man Christ Jesus; Who gave himself a ransom for all, to be testified in due time."* **1 Timothy 2:5-6**

It won't be a surprise that the picture prophet John had in mind when he saw the Lord Jesus coming was Exodus 12, which speaks of the deliverance of the nation of Israel from Egypt by reason of the Passover lamb. The blood of those lambs became their means of safety from the destroyer and their exit from years of cruel bondage under the whip of Pharaoh and his taskmasters. As those Passover lambs were slain to deliver them, so also the blood of Jesus Christ, our Passover Lamb, has been sacrifice for our deliverance.

> *"Purge out therefore the old leaven, that ye may be a new lump, as ye are unleavened. For even Christ our passover is sacrificed for us:"*
> **1 Corinthians 5:7.**

Christ is not called a Lamb because He is one literally; rather, He is referred to as a Lamb because of His role in redemption. He is Elohim Eternal Word, equal in essence with Elohim. He only became flesh for the purpose of providing a perfect blood to purchase us from sin and Satan's hold. The just requirement or price for grace was a perfect, sinless, and superior blood that could take away the sin of mankind once and for all time. Since there was none who could provide such pure needed blood, God, out of love, volunteered Himself. Since God is a Spirit and has no blood, He had to become a man. God becoming a man was the only way out. In His infinite mercies, He did and His name is JESUS – bless His holy name! By virtue of Him laying down His life, His Soul was poured out as a sin offering for humanity, affording Him the title: 'The Lamb of God'.

Now! Do you have any earthly ideal of what it means for the Eternal God to be born as a mortal man or son of man with all its limitations? Have you ever thought of what it must have meant for Him, the King of Glory, to be born in a manger? No earthly king would allow their son or daughter to be born in such a degrading state. Yet the King of the Heavens and Earth allowed His Son to be born amongst the lambs, in order that He might identify with the lambs. This is humility of the greatest order and a price He paid for grace. Grace is free but wasn't cheap. It cost Heaven His best.

> *"But as he which hath called you is holy, so be ye holy in all manner of conversation; Because it is written, Be ye holy; for I am holy. And if ye call on the Father, who without respect of persons judgeth according to every man's work, pass the time of your sojourning here in fear: Forasmuch as ye know that ye were not redeemed with corruptible things, as silver and gold, from your vain conversation received by tradition from your fathers; But with the precious blood of Christ, as of a lamb without blemish and without spot: Who verily was foreordained before the foundation of the world, but was manifest in these last times for you,"* **1 Peter 1:15-20**

THE COST

In this passage of scripture, the Holy Spirit through His servant is admonishing us to be separate and distinct from the world, which is what it simply means to be holy. He further warns all who call God Father to live a godly life, for the inevitable reason that He is going to judge every man's work. Then, he reminded his audience as well as us what it cost Yahweh to redeemed us and what He has redeemed us from. To be redeemed is to be bought back or rescued by a ransom. Yes! Yahweh has rescued and bought us back to Himself not by silver or gold (representing earthly resources) but by the precious blood of Christ, as of a Lamb without blemish and without spot.

The Greek word translated precious here is '*Timios*', pronounce as '*Tim-ee-os*', meaning: *costly, honoured, esteemed, valuable, very dear, accounted as of great price*. This proves clearly that the blood of Christ by which we have been ransomed is very dear and costly; it is of great price; it is highly esteemed; it is most honourable and valuable. This is the most costly price paid by Christ for us to access grace freely. Holy Spirit has specifically chosen these words to remind the saints of the high cost of their redemption, so they do not lightly esteem the blood of Christ shed for them. The blood of Christ is a heavenly jewel of inestimable and incalculable value.

> *"And from Jesus Christ, who is the faithful witness, and the first begotten of the dead, and the prince of the kings of the earth. Unto him that loved us, and washed us from our sins in his own blood, And hath made us kings and priests unto God and his Father; to him be glory and dominion for ever and ever. Amen."* **Revelation 1:5-6**

> *"And [now] they sing a new song, saying, You are worthy to take the scroll and to break the seals that are on it, for You were slain (sacrificed), and with Your blood You purchased men unto God from every tribe and language and*

people and nation. And You have made them a kingdom (royal race) and priests to our God, and they shall reign [as kings] over the earth!" **Revelation 5:9-10 Amplified Bible.**

Through the blood of Jesus Christ shed for us on the cross, He has loosed and freed us from our sins. The Amplified version of Revelation chapter 5:10 says: He was slain or sacrificed, and with His blood He purchased men unto God from every tribe and language and people and nation. That, my dear friends and readers, is the cost of grace. We have been purchased by the precious, costly blood of Christ as our Passover Lamb.

Time and Utility Consumed – His Life

"I am the good shepherd: the good shepherd giveth his life for the sheep…Therefore doth my Father love me, because I lay down my life, that I might take it again. No man taketh it

from me, but I lay it down of myself. I have power to lay it down, and I have power to take it again. This commandment have I received of my Father." **John 10:11,17-18**

"Greater love hath no man than this, that a man lay down his life for his friends." **John 15:13**

God is not an irrational being but a rational, intelligent being. He is a God of Process and operates according to His law of process. God has all it takes and could have created the heavens and the earth and everything in it in one day; but He did not, and so, allowed the law of process to be effected. He created the earth in six days and rested the seventh day. In the same vein, when Adam and Eve sinned and fell, God had the power to instantly put into effect their redemption and complete it before Adam died; yet He didn't, but applied the law of process.

The Lamb of God slain before the foundation of the

THE COST

world would not manifest until the fullness of time came. I have come to realize that in God dealing with us, He acts according to the law of process. He does not and may not give us the breakthrough that we need until all things are ready. By all things I mean the right environment, friends, destiny helpers, etc. Most times, you may be fit and ready to go but God may not let you because your spouse or children or family or friends are not ready. Elijah did not call fire, and fire did not just fall from heaven until the altar was repaired and fully placed in order.

Moreover, the Lord instructed Moses to command the people on the particular day to select the Passover lamb and a particular day to slay the lamb. Our God is definitely not a God of confusion but of process and order. In the verse above, the Lord addressed Himself as the good shepherd who laid His life down for the sheep. Wow! What a statement! What does He mean by laying down His life for the sheep? It simply means He exchange His life for the life of the sheep. He died in place of the sheep, so that the sheep will no longer die but live forever with

Him eternally. His death was not a suicide, neither was He crucified for nothing. He of His own free will laid down His life for us that we might have and live His life.

This is the reason He is the good shepherd: because He cared affectionately for His lost and scattered sheep and willingly lay aside His glory, took upon the form of a man, suffered selflessly, and died a shameful death of a notorious criminal on the cross. His life has been cut short for us to live eternally. Note what He implied in John 10:17-18: His life was not taken from Him. No! He laid it down on His own accord in harmony with His Father's commandments. In order words, the Father had already declared unto Him what the cost of grace would be and He said to the Father; it's expensive but I am willing to pay it in full. Thank God He did pay in full. To Him, it wasn't easy, but it was worth it.

> "Now is my soul troubled; and what shall I say? Father, save me from this hour: but for this cause came I unto this

hour. Father, glorify thy name. Then came there a voice from heaven, saying, I have both glorified it, and will glorify it again." **John 12:27-28**

Risk Incurred – His Temptations, Humiliations and Rejections

"I am the Good Shepherd. The Good Shepherd risks and lays down His [own] life for the sheep." **John 10:11 (Amplified Bible)**

From the onset of the promise of the Messiah, who is the ultimate Seed of the woman, ordained to bruise the head of Satan, God made it clear that the serpent was going to bruise His heel. This the serpent did quite well, never directly but indirectly through human vessels that yielded themselves to his deceptive schemes. Those bruises ranged from Christ's humble birth to His humiliating death on the cross as foretold by God through His prophets of old. Most of us may not understand that God's mission to be born as man for the purpose of redemption was a great risk on His part.

> *"Ought not Christ to have suffered these things, and to enter into his glory? And beginning at Moses and all the prophets, he expounded unto them in all the scriptures the things concerning himself."* **Luke 24:26-27.**

Someone may wonder, what risk could there be for God? My response to that is: was there a risk involved when God created Adam? Of course yes! Then, if there was a risk at that point, certainly there was a risk when God became a man. As the first Adam fell, the second Adam could have also fallen, but, God be praised, He didn't. I am sure that statement might upset someone's theology. So, let me prove it by asking this question: did Christ function as God on earth or as a man? Obviously, He functioned as a sinless man anointed by the Holy Spirit without measure. He constantly referred to Himself as the Son of man. Here is my point: if He had functioned as God, His temptation by the tempter would have been a flop and unfair to humans and unjustifiable.

For He was tempted with evil and the scriptures says in James 1:13 that God cannot be tempted with evil, hence, He had to be tempted as a man. As a man, He was subjected to the same temptation as you and I. The scripture says in Hebrews 4:15 that He was in all points tempted as we are, yet without sin. This, my dear readers, was a risk that God was willing to take as a high cost of grace.

You see, when God became a man for the sake of grace, He became limited as a person living in a falling world. According to Hebrew 2:14-15: He took upon Himself flesh and blood, that through death He might destroy Satan who had the power of death, and deliver humanity from Satan's bondage fostered by fear. As a partaker of flesh and blood, He became subject to legitimate human needs and temptations. He was hungry, tired, sleepy, thirsty, and vulnerable like every other man. This is one of the major reasons the Jewish leaders of His day rejected Him. He was regular; there was nothing physically special about Him as the prophets foretold.

> *"For [the Servant of God] grew up before Him like a tender plant, and like a root out of dry ground; He has no form or comeliness [royal, kingly pomp], that we should look at Him, and no beauty that we should desire Him."*
> **Isaiah 53:2 (Amplified Bible)**

In anticipation of the Messiah, they expected someone of royal status; dignity or military-might to rescue them from the oppressing rod of foreign invaders. As a result, they judged the gift by the package and missed it. To this, John 1:11 testifies: *"He came to His own, and His own received Him not"*. God sending His Son in this lowly manner was a calculable risk in humility. It's not weakness as the Jews supposed, neither is it foolishness as the Greeks infer, but it was God using the foolish things of this world to confound the wise and using the seemingly weak things to bring to naught the vain things that are highly esteemed by men. God's gracious act of humility in the work of grace was designed to humble the exalted and exalt the humble.

Opportunity Foregone – He Set Aside His Divinity

"Let this mind be in you, which was also in Christ Jesus: Who, being in the form of God, thought it not robbery to be equal with God: But made himself of no reputation, and took upon him the form of a servant, and was made in the likeness of men: And being found in fashion as a man, he humbled himself, and became obedient unto death, even the death of the cross. Wherefore God also hath highly exalted him, and given him a name which is above every name: That at the name of Jesus every knee should bow, of things in

heaven, and things in earth, and things under the earth; And that every tongue should confess that Jesus Christ is Lord, to the glory of God the Father." **Philippians 2:5-11**

"I have glorified thee on the earth: I have finished the work which thou gavest me to do. And now, O Father, glorify thou me with thine own self with the glory which I had with thee before the world was." **John 17:4-5**

Since cost includes opportunities foregone or what one gives up in order to get something, all that Christ gave up in order to make grace available and accessible is the high cost of grace. In the passage above, we are made aware what Christ gave up to purchase our salvation. Although He possessed the fullness of the attributes which make God, God, He selflessly set aside His deity and stripped Himself of all privileges and rightful dignity to take the form of a servant. Can you fathom that? Even if we are able to gamble with the concept of why God became a man, how do we reconcile the idea of God becoming a servant for man's sake? This is too much for our minds to understand.

As if that was not enough, the scripture says He abased and humbled Himself furthermore and became obedient to the extreme of death as a common criminal. This gracious act of God is mind-boggling and beyond human comprehension. This proves the psalmist right who says 'we will never know how much it cost to see our sins upon the cross'. All we can comprehend by faith on this side of eternity is only but a fragment of the whole cost of grace. This is a true picture of the cost of grace, that God stooped so low to die and purchase our pardon. He is truly gracious!

Therefore, because the Lord stooped so low, God has highly exalted Him and freely bestowed on Him the name that is above every other name, which translate to salvation by grace through faith in His name.

Further Detailed Analyses of the Cost

"Then he said unto them, O fools, and slow of heart to believe all that the prophets have spoken: Ought not Christ to have suffered these things, and to enter into his glory? And beginning at Moses and all the prophets, he expounded unto them in all the scriptures the things concerning himself." **Luke 24: 25-27**

So far, our discussion has been an overview of the divine fixed variable or factors in the revealed cost of grace. Using the definition of cost in business terms, we have discussed the heavenly effort involved; the material as His body broken for us; the resource as His bloodshed for us; time and utility consumed as the law of process and His life cut short for our sins; risk incurred as His temptation, humiliations, and rejections; and opportunities foregone as the setting aside of His deity to become a servant. As enlightened as this may be, they are but a scratch in the surface of how deep a price was paid for our salvation. Hence, the intention here is to dig further and describe in graphic detail – as best as possible – all that the Lord Jesus went through from His birth to His ascension, as foretold by the prophets in the Old Testament, fulfilled by Him in the New Testament.

The Risk and Danger of His Birth

"And when they were departed, behold, the angel of the Lord appeareth to Joseph in a dream, saying, Arise, and take the young child and his mother, and flee into Egypt, and be thou there until I bring thee word: for Herod will seek the young child to destroy him. When he arose, he took the young child and his mother by night, and departed into Egypt: And was there until the death of Herod: that it might be fulfilled which was spoken of the Lord by the

prophet, saying, Out of Egypt have I called my son." **Matthew 2:13-15**

Sufficient cost is the humble circumstances of His birth in a manger. We are not referring to the birth of a child to the poorest outcasts in Israel, but the birth of the Son of God – King of the Jews. We have no record of anyone else ever born in such a place throughout the Bible. If I was God, I probably wouldn't have done that, would you? I am glad God is not like man; He is infinitely merciful and gracious. This was the price He had to pay for grace. To add insult to injury, king Herod being threatened at the news of a new king's birth planned to kill the young child before He even had the chance to live. Except for the intervention of Heaven, Herod would have killed Him as he did other innocent children.

His Temptations

"Then was Jesus led up of the Spirit into the wilderness to be tempted of the

THE COST

devil. And when he had fasted forty days and forty nights, he was afterward an hungred. And when the tempter came to him, he said, If thou be the Son of God, command that these stones be made bread. But he answered and said, It is written, Man shall not live by bread alone, but by every word that proceedeth out of the mouth of God. Then the devil taketh him up into the holy city, and setteth him on a pinnacle of the temple, And saith unto him, If thou be the Son of God, cast thyself down: for it is written, He shall give his angels charge concerning thee: and in their hands they shall bear thee up, lest at any time thou dash thy foot against a stone. Jesus said unto him, It is written again, Thou shalt not tempt the Lord thy God. Again, the devil taketh him up into an exceeding high mountain, and sheweth him all the kingdoms of the

> *world, and the glory of them; And saith unto him, All these things will I give thee, if thou wilt fall down and worship me. Then saith Jesus unto him, Get thee hence, Satan: for it is written, Thou shalt worship the Lord thy God, and him only shalt thou serve. Then the devil leaveth him, and, behold, angels came and ministered unto him."*
> **Matthew 4:1-11**

As discussed earlier, the Lord Jesus did not function as God in the flesh but as man with flesh and blood. He was subject to temptations as much as Adam was. He could have fallen to the tempter, had He chose to do so. If He couldn't have fallen, then it would have been no temptation at all. You can't subject a blind man to temptation with a naked woman; it wouldn't be a temptation. He was indeed tempted in all points but did not sin. Overcoming the temptation of the devil was part of the price He had to pay for grace.

THE COST

The Price of Rejections from Jewish Leaders

"Then came the officers to the chief priests and Pharisees; and they said unto them, Why have ye not brought him? The officers answered, Never man spake like this man. Then answered them the Pharisees, Are ye also deceived? Have any of the rulers or of the Pharisees believed on him?" **John 7:45-48**

"They answered and said unto him, Abraham is our father. Jesus saith unto them, If ye were Abraham's children, ye would do the works of Abraham. But now ye seek to kill me, a man that hath told you the truth, which I have heard of God: this did not Abraham." **John 8:39-40**

Rejection is the act of spurning a person's affections (1Peter 2:4). It is also an act of dismissing or refusing a proposal. This is what the Jewish leaders did to Christ; they dismissed His affections and refused His message of Salvation. Was Christ affected by the rejection? Yes, of course! He was deeply affected; as flesh and blood He was hurt. He was affected to the point of lamentation as He wept over Jerusalem:

> *"O Jerusalem, Jerusalem, which killest the prophets, and stonest them that are sent unto thee; how often would I have gathered thy children together, as a hen doth gather her brood under her wings, and ye would not! Behold, your house is left unto you desolate: and verily I say unto you, Ye shall not see me, until the time come when ye shall say, Blessed is he that cometh in the name of the Lord."* **Luke 13:34-35**

Every one of us could certainly identify with the pain of rejection, one way or the other. It is one of the worst psychological pains that can be inflicted on our emotions. It comes with all kinds of negative effects. Fear of rejection is the leading cause of compromise amongst young and old, especially the today teenager. It amounts to peer-pressure in our today political correctness era. In regards to Christ, it was foretold in Isaiah 52:2 that He would be despised and rejected by men. And so it was; He was rejected that we might be accepted. He was disallowed of men so that we might be allowed by God.

> *"These words spake his parents, because they feared the Jews: for the Jews had agreed already, that if any man did confess that he was Christ, he should be put out of the synagogue. Therefore said his parents, He is of age; ask him. Then again called they the man that was blind, and said unto him, Give God the praise: we know that this man is a sinner. He answered and said, Whether he be a sinner or no, I know not: one thing I know, that,*

whereas I was blind, now I see. Then said they to him again, What did he to thee? how opened he thine eyes? He answered them, I have told you already, and ye did not hear: wherefore would ye hear it again? will ye also be his disciples? Then they reviled him, and said, Thou art his disciple; but we are Moses' disciples. We know that God spake unto Moses: as for this fellow, we know not from whence he is." **John 9:22-29**

He was not only rejected by the leaders, but the very people to whom He came to die rejected Him. Even the Roman authority discarded Him (John 11:48). They out-rightly dismissed, disapproved, and opposed His message.

The Price of Betray

"When Jesus had thus said, he was troubled in spirit, and testified, and

THE COST

said, Verily, verily, I say unto you, that one of you shall betray me." **John 13:21**

"Yea, mine own familiar friend, in whom I trusted, which did eat of my bread, hath lifted up his heel against me." **Psalm 41:9**

"And while he yet spake, lo, Judas, one of the twelve, came, and with him a great multitude with swords and staves, from the chief priests and elders of the people. Now he that betrayed him gave them a sign, saying, Whomsoever I shall kiss, that same is he: hold him fast. And forthwith he came to Jesus, and said, Hail, master; and kissed him. And Jesus said unto him, Friend, wherefore art thou come? Then came they, and laid hands on Jesus, and took him." **Matthew 26:47-50**

THE COST OF GRACE

"But Jesus said unto him, Judas, betrayest thou the Son of man with a kiss?" **Luke 22:48**

Have you ever felt the pain of being betrayed by a friend or close relative? Have you ever had someone give you over just for personal gain or a favour? It is so painful, we can all agree. This is what some of those the Lord handpicked to be His followers did to Him: what a high cost of grace indeed! I used to wonder about Judas' act of betrayal; I couldn't really comprehend it until I saw it in Luke 22:1-6. I understood as much as the Pharisees, chief priests, and scribes wanting Jesus dead, but didn't know how they could accomplish their conspiracy without an uproar by the people.

Since they were faced with that dilemma, Judas Iscariot aid and abet was a perfect plan on how to execute their satanic conspiracy. The scripture said *"they were glad and covenanted to give him money"*. And in turn, he promised and sought opportunity to betray Him unto them in the absence of the multitude. The fact that they were delighted shows how great a deal his strategy to betray Jesus into their hands was. Thank God it was the price paid for our redemption. His betrayal meant our deliverance from the betrayal of Adam and Eve's betrayer.

> "When the morning was come, all the chief priests and elders of the people took counsel against Jesus to put him to death: And when they had bound him, they led him away, and delivered him to Pontius Pilate the governor. Then Judas, which had betrayed him, when he saw that he was condemned, repented himself, and brought again the thirty pieces of silver to the chief priests and elders, Saying, I have sinned in that I have betrayed the innocent blood. And they said, What is that to us? see thou to that. And he cast down the pieces of silver in the temple, and departed, and went and hanged

himself. And the chief priests took the silver pieces, and said, It is not lawful for to put them into the treasury, because it is the price of blood. And they took counsel, and bought with them the potter's field, to bury strangers in. Wherefore that field was called, The field of blood, unto this day. Then was fulfilled that which was spoken by Jeremy the prophet, saying, And they took the thirty pieces of silver, the price of him that was valued, whom they of the children of Israel did value; And gave them for the potter's field, as the Lord appointed me." **Matthew 27:1-10.**

The Price of Being Denied and Forsaken

"And the Lord said, Simon, Simon, behold, Satan hath desired to have you, that he may sift you as wheat: But I have prayed for thee, that thy faith fail not: and when thou art converted,

THE COST

strengthen thy brethren. And he said unto him, Lord, I am ready to go with thee, both into prison, and to death. And he said, I tell thee, Peter, the cock shall not crow this day, before that thou shalt thrice deny that thou knowest me... Then took they him, and led him, and brought him into the high priest's house. And Peter followed afar off. And when they had kindled a fire in the midst of the hall, and were set down together, Peter sat down among them. But a certain maid beheld him as he sat by the fire, and earnestly looked upon him, and said, This man was also with him. And he denied him, saying, Woman, I know him not. And after a little while another saw him, and said, Thou art also of them. And Peter said, Man, I am not. And about the space of one hour after another confidently affirmed, saying, Of a truth this fellow also was with him: for he is a Galilaean. And Peter said, Man, I know not what thou sayest. And immediately, while he yet spake, the cock crew. And the Lord turned, and looked upon Peter. And Peter remembered the word of the Lord, how he had said unto him, Before the cock crow, thou shalt deny me thrice. And Peter went out, and wept bitterly." **Luke 22:31-34, 54-62**

"And they all forsook him, and fled." **Mark 14:50**

"But all this was done, that the scriptures of the prophets might be fulfilled. Then all the disciples forsook him, and fled." **Matthew 26:56**

The incidents recorded in these preceding verses of scripture might seem insignificant to casual observers, but in reality, they are not. If these incidents where insignificant, why would God described them prophetically in details under the Old Covenant? Beside the fact that they are signs of the suffering Messiah, every one of these reproaches against the Lord were ordained by God to specifically fulfil a part in the overall work of redemption. How would you feel if someone you eat and drink with suddenly claims they don't even know you on the day of your adversity, when you probably needed their company the most? It is devastating and demoralizing. It has the potential to drain the little strength one may have left to face their trials.

May those who are supposed to help us not desert us in the day of trials as Disciple Peter did to Jesus His Master. Often times, some of us wrongly assume it was only Peter who denied the Lord and only Judas betrayed Him. The fact check in Mark 11:50 proves otherwise. It shows that when He was arrested in the garden of Gethsemane, all the disciples forsook Him and fled; these actions are also equal to betrayal. The only difference between Judas' actions, and Peter and the rest of the disciples' actions, in my opinion, is the difference between cold blooded murderer and manslaughter. Although they may both have killed someone, nevertheless, their motives are completely different. The former conspired, schemed, and executed the plan; while the latter usually happens accidentally in the heat of the moment without a premeditated plan. While Judas acted with a personal agenda and self-profit, Peter and the rest of the disciples acted from a personal weakness, unintended.

In any case, it was part of the price the Lord had to pay as our ransom. Christ was denied so that God the Father would not have to deny us. He was forsaken so that we might be accepted of the Father. Bless His holy name!

The Cruel Price of Mockery

"And the men that held Jesus mocked him, and smote him. And when they had blindfolded him, they struck him on the face, and asked him, saying,

THE COST

Prophesy, who is it that smote thee? And many other things blasphemously spake they against him." **Luke 22:63-65**

"And Herod with his men of war set him at nought, and mocked him, and arrayed him in a gorgeous robe, and sent him again to Pilate." **Luke 23:11**

In light of this passage, the question to be asked is: did the Lord Jesus deserve to be mocked in this unwarranted manner? Of course not! But why did He have to go through all this? The answer to that is found in the prophecy of Isaiah 53: *'for the transgression of my people was he stricken...'* This is the mockery that we deserved falling on him. I wonder why the people were not afraid to mock Him, let alone beat Him. It's obvious. They were under the heavy influence of Satan, as the Lord alluded in verse 53: that this is their hour and the power of darkness.

They scoffed, ridiculed, blindfolded, and slapped

Him, demanding that he prophesy who slapped Him. To act in this fashion toward a criminal would be considered extreme torture, let alone the sinless Son of the Highest. This is the high cost of grace indeed! This mockery was done at the high priest palace (Matthew 26:57) by their own guard, not the Romans. After being mocked in the high priest palace, He was taken in chains to Pontius Pilate, the governor, where the soldiers of the governor did their worst mockeries of Him.

> *"Then the soldiers of the governor took Jesus into the common hall, and gathered unto him the whole band of soldiers. And they stripped him, and put on him a scarlet robe. And when they had platted a crown of thorns, they put it upon his head, and a reed in his right hand: and they bowed the knee before him, and mocked him, saying, Hail, King of the Jews! And they spit upon him, and took the reed, and smote him on the head. And after that they had*

mocked him, they took the robe off from him, and put his own raiment on him, and led him away to crucify him."
Matthew 27:27-31

Here we see how the Roman soldiers made fun of their creator. They stripped Him of His clothes and put a scarlet robe on Him, put a crown of thorns on His head, a staff on His hand, and kneeling before Him, they made spot of Him. I wonder what He must have felt watching them do this to Him. A lamb dumped before the sharers indeed. More-so, He was mocked by King Herod and his men (see Luke 23:11 Amplified Version). The Scripture says: "And Herod with His men of war set him at nought", meaning they ridiculed and scoffed Him.

His Exchange for Barabas

"But the chief priests and elders persuaded the multitude that they should ask Barabbas, and destroy Jesus. The governor answered and said

unto them, Whether of the twain will ye that I release unto you? They said, Barabbas. Pilate saith unto them, What shall I do then with Jesus which is called Christ? They all say unto him, Let him be crucified. And the governor said, Why, what evil hath he done? But they cried out the more, saying, Let him be crucified. When Pilate saw that he could prevail nothing, but that rather a tumult was made, he took water, and washed his hands before the multitude, saying, I am innocent of the blood of this just person: see ye to it. Then answered all the people, and said, His blood be on us, and on our children. Then released he Barabbas unto them: and when he had scourged Jesus, he delivered him to be crucified." Matthew 27: 20-26

"And they cried out all at once, saying, Away with this man, and release unto

THE COST

us Barabbas: (Who for a certain sedition made in the city, and for murder, was cast into prison.) Pilate therefore, willing to release Jesus, spake again to them. But they cried, saying, Crucify him, crucify him. And he said unto them the third time, Why, what evil hath he done? I have found no cause of death in him: I will therefore chastise him, and let him go. And they were instant with loud voices, requiring that he might be crucified. And the voices of them and of the chief priests prevailed. And Pilate gave sentence that it should be as they required. And he released unto them him that for sedition and murder was cast into prison, whom they had desired; but he delivered Jesus to their will." **Luke 23:18-25**

This is a perfect illustration of the price for grace:

the just for the unjust, the guiltless in exchange for the guilty. As the chief priest and elders persuaded the multitude to ask for Barabas and destroy Jesus, even more-so had the Father persuaded Christ to take our place in death so that we might be released from the prison of sin and Satan. This is the greater exchange: He that knew no sin became sin for us, that we might be made the righteousness of God in Him. We were all Barabas who has been exchanged with Christ for God. This is G-R-A-C-E: GOD'S-RICHES-AT-CHRIST'S-EXPENSE. The reason His accusers preferred the unjust Barabas above the just and Holy One is because it was ordained by God to be so, that we might be justified by His grace.

Note that, not only did the people prefer Barabas to Christ; the leaders also preferred Caesar over Jesus. They declared openly that they had no king but Caesar.

> *"And it was the preparation of the passover, and about the sixth hour: and*

he saith unto the Jews, Behold your King! But they cried out, Away with him, away with him, crucify him. Pilate saith unto them, Shall I crucify your King? The chief priests answered, We have no king but Caesar." **John 19:14-15.**

They Labeled Him a Sinner

"Then again called they the man that was blind, and said unto him, Give God the praise: we know that this man is a sinner." **John 9:24**

What is the point of this, one may wonder? The point is that this was a scandal and a blackmail of the highest order. It's a character assassination and a deformation of character. To call a sinless and a Just One a sinner openly and publicly is a discredit to His Holy reputation. How would you feel? Or what would you do when you are wrongly labelled with a crime that you hadn't even thought of, let alone committed. It can be painful and devastating. In

Luke 15:2, they began by accusing Him of receiving and eating with sinners. In Luke 7:34, they proceeded to label Him friend of sinners. In John 9:24, they openly labelled Him a sinner. What an irony, sinners calling the sinless one a sinner. This is surely one such bundle of contradictions from sinners the Lord endured against Himself in order to purchase our pardon.

The Agony at Gethsemane

"And they came to a place which was named Gethsemane: and he saith to his disciples, Sit ye here, while I shall pray. And he taketh with him Peter and James and John, and began to be sore amazed, and to be very heavy; And saith unto them, My soul is exceeding sorrowful unto death: tarry ye here, and watch. And he went forward a little, and fell on the ground, and prayed that, if it were possible, the hour might pass

THE COST

from him. And he said, Abba, Father, all things are possible unto thee; take away this cup from me: nevertheless not what I will, but what thou wilt. And he cometh, and findeth them sleeping, and saith unto Peter, Simon, sleepest thou? couldest not thou watch one hour? Watch ye and pray, lest ye enter into temptation. The spirit truly is ready, but the flesh is weak. And again he went away, and prayed, and spake the same words. And when he returned, he found them asleep again, (for their eyes were heavy,) neither wist they what to answer him. And he cometh the third time, and saith unto them, Sleep on now, and take your rest: it is enough, the hour is come; behold, the Son of man is betrayed into the hands of sinners. Rise up, let us go; lo, he that betrayeth me is at hand." **Mark 14:32-42**

"And He took with Him Peter and James and John, and began to be struck with terror and amazement and deeply troubled and depressed. And He said to them, My soul is exceedingly sad (overwhelmed with grief) so that it almost kills Me! Remain here and keep awake and be watching." **Mark 33-34 (Amplified Bible)**

"And being in an agony [of mind], He prayed [all the] more earnestly and intently, and His sweat became like great clots of blood dropping down upon the ground." **Luke 22:44 (Amplified Bible)**

"Then Jesus went with them to a place called Gethsemane, and He told His disciples, Sit down here while I go over yonder and pray. And taking with Him Peter and the two sons of Zebedee, He began to show grief and distress of

> *mind and was deeply depressed. Then He said to them, My soul is very sad and deeply grieved, so that I am almost dying of sorrow. Stay here and keep awake and keep watch with Me."*
> **Matthew 26:36-38 (Amplified Bible)**

Often times, some of us read through these scriptures but do not consider them in depth. Hence, we sometimes miss the magnitude of what it cost the Lord to ransom us from sin and Satan's dominion. While Christ was in prayer at the garden of Gethsemane, the above scriptures unveiled to us His state of anguish. Note the various vocabularies used by the writer of the gospels: He was in agony of mind; He began to be sorrowful and very heavy. He said Himself; *"My soul is exceedingly sorrowful"*. According to the Amplified Bible; He began to show grief and distress of the mind and was deeply depressed. Then He said, *"My soul is very sad and deeply grieved, so that I am almost dying of sorrow."* This is proof that the cross was not a joyful ride for the Lord; neither should we take the cross lightly.

Mark 14:33 says that: *"He began to be sore amazed and to be very heavy."* The Amplified Bible rendered that phrase as: He began to be struck with terror and amazement and deeply troubled in prayer before His Father." The account of Luke in chapter 22:44 gave us a deeper perspective of the suffering of Christ in Gethsemane. It stated that Christ was in an agony of the mind, He prayed all the more earnestly and intently, and His sweat became like great clots of blood dropping down upon the ground. What travail and groaning He must have endured. No doubt this is what the author of the book of Hebrews interprets as 'resisting unto blood'. His anguish of soul was that we might no longer languish in sin and sickness. Glory to His name!

The Price of Dishonour

"Jesus answered, I have not a devil; but I honour my Father, and ye do

dishonour me." **John 8:49**

The Lord would never lie or play with words. If the Lord says He is dishonoured, it simply means He was dishonoured indeed. The word translated as 'dishonoured' here simply means to be lowered down from the place of honour; indignity; to be treated disgracefully or shamed. These definitions give us insight into how the Lord truly felt about their whole treatment of Him. He felt lowered down from the place of honour by them. He felt treated disgracefully and shamefully by them. He felt vilify, despised, and scorned; and yet the Lord was not bitter because He understood that it was the price He came to pay.

The Price of Spit

> *"And they spit upon him, and took the reed, and smote him on the head."* **Matthew 27:30**

> *"And some began to spit on him, and to cover his face, and to buffet him, and to*

say unto him, Prophesy: and the servants did strike him with the palms of their hands." **Mark 14:65**

"Then did they spit in his face, and buffeted him; and others smote him with the palms of their hands," **Matthew 26:67**

As we all would agree, deliberately spitting on someone is considered rude and a social taboo in all cultures of the world. It is a universal sign of anger, hatred, contempt, or disrespect. It is quite obvious from this context that those who spat on the Lord Jesus were vulgarly expressing their hatred, anger, disrespect, or contempt of Him. Then, the inevitable question asked by Pilate was: why? What evil has He done? Even Pilate found no offence in Him. Therefore, His only offence was that He had willingly and voluntary surrendered Himself to God as our scapegoat.

I am persuaded that this entire disdainful act that was been done to Him was the Father laying on Him

THE COST

the iniquity of us all. A casual look at our text above would make it seem that the Lord was spat on by the same people, but that wasn't the case. He was spat on and mocked twice by two different groups of folks. First, at the chief priest palace, possibly by the guard who arrested Him and some of the council members (Matthew26:57, 65-68). Secondly, at Pontius Pilate's palace, by the governor's soldiers (Matthew 27:1-2; 27-30). Interestingly, both Jews and Gentiles spat on Him, which represents the religious rulers and the political rulers showing their hatred for no cause, only so that the scripture might be fulfilled which says: "They hated me without a cause."

> *"He that hateth me hateth my Father also. If I had not done among them the works which none other man did, they had not had sin: but now have they both seen and hated both me and my Father. But this cometh to pass, that the word might be fulfilled that is written in*

their law, They hated me without a cause." **John 15:23-25.**

"They rewarded me evil for good to the spoiling of my soul." **Psalm 35:12.**

To me personally, this is the depth of humiliation, for vile men to spit on the face of an innocent and guiltless Son of God, who had done nothing but good only, is beyond comprehension.

The Price of Beaten

"Then did they spit in his face, and buffeted him; and others smote him with the palms of their hands, Saying, Prophesy unto us, thou Christ, Who is he that smote thee?" **Matthew 26:67-68**

From the moment the Priest guards arrested the Lord Jesus, they began maltreating Him. In the chief priest palace, He was beaten as well as in the Pontius Pilate's Palace. It is needful to highlight and analyse the various words used by the four writers of the four Gospels to describe His cruel manhandling and beatings.

Scourged:

> *"Then Pilate therefore took Jesus, and scourged him. And the soldiers platted a crown of thorns, and put it on his head, and they put on him a purple robe, And said, Hail, King of the Jews! and they smote him with their hands."*
> **John 19:1-3.**

To scourge is to whip – that is, to lash as a public punishment. The Jewish method of scourging was by the use of three thongs of leather. The offender receives thirteen stripes on the bare breast and thirteen on each shoulder, making thirty-nine stripes. Meanwhile, under the Roman method of scourging, the person was stripped and tied in a bending posture to a pillar or stretched on a frame. The scourge was made of leather thongs, weighted with sharp pieces of bone or lead, which tore the flesh of both the back and the breast. The Lord Jesus suffered this cruel, inhumane scourging by both the Jewish and Roman hands.

Thank God for the movie *"The Passion of The Christ"*, which is the only movie of Christ ever made that truly reflects the suffering of Christ. Most critics of the movie felt that the torture of Christ was exaggerated, that the brutality should have been tone down. But, according to the foretold prophecy, His punishment had to be as brutal as seen on the film. The scripture foretold that He would be beaten beyond recognition:

> *"As many were astonied at thee; his visage was so marred more than any man, and his form more than the sons of men:"* **Isaiah 52:14.**

The Amplified Bible says He became an object of horror. In other words, He was so beaten, battered, and bruised to the point that He became deformed and disfigured. This is also in fulfilment of the prophecy in Isaiah 53:5, which says: *"… He was wounded for our transgression and bruised for our iniquities…"* All these He willingly endured as a price to be paid for the grace that brings salvation to us all.

Stroke:

Luke 22:64 says they *"stroke him on the face…"* Simply put, they struck Him on His face. To strike means to deal a blow, or to hit forcibly and deliberately with one's hand or a weapon. In light of our definition, it is obvious how the Lord Jesus was hit forcibly and deliberately with a blow on His face.

Smite:

> *"And the men that held Jesus mocked him, and smote him. And when they had blindfolded him, they struck him on the face, and asked him, saying, Prophesy, who is it that smote thee?"*
> **Luke 22:63-64**

To smite or smote is to slap: that is, strike with the palm of the hand. It could also be a blow with the hand or rod. This is what the high priest attendants did to the Master. They slapped Him, struck Him with a blow, and teased Him to prophesy who slapped Him. In regards to the cruel Roman soldiers, they did not only slap Him, but smote and struck His head with a staff.

Buffeted:

"Then did they spit in his face, and buffeted him; and others smote him with the palms of their hands," **Matthew 26:67.**

"And some began to spit on him, and to cover his face, and to buffet him, and to say unto him, Prophesy: and the servants did strike him with the palms of their hands." **Mark 14:65**

To buffet someone is to strike with clenched hands or to punch with a fist. It also means to strike repeatedly and violently; to batter; to pound; to afflict someone over a long period; to cause trouble or suffering to someone. The Greek word translated as 'buffet' has an image of a ragging sea consistently beating against the coast rocks. I am sure you get the picture? All these and more are the kinds of violent assaults the Lord Jesus endured as the ransom for grace. He was consistently and violently punched, struck, battered, and pounded from His point of arrest to being hanged on the cross – all for grace!

The Price of Nakedness

> *"Then released he Barabbas unto them: and when he had scourged Jesus, he delivered him to be crucified. Then the soldiers of the governor took Jesus into the common hall, and gathered unto him the whole band of soldiers. And they stripped him, and put on him a scarlet robe. And when they had platted a crown of thorns, they put it upon his*

head, and a reed in his right hand: and they bowed the knee before him, and mocked him, saying, Hail, King of the Jews! And they spit upon him, and took the reed, and smote him on the head. And after that they had mocked him, they took the robe off from him, and put his own raiment on him, and led him away to crucify him." **Matthew 27:26-31.**

"Then the soldiers, when they had crucified Jesus, took his garments, and made four parts, to every soldier a part; and also his coat: now the coat was without seam, woven from the top throughout. They said therefore among themselves, Let us not rend it, but cast lots for it, whose it shall be: that the scripture might be fulfilled, which saith, They parted my raiment among them, and for my vesture they did cast lots.

THE COST

These things therefore the soldiers did."
John 19:24

To strip is to take off all covering. Hence, to strip someone is to take off all their clothing and leave them naked. The Scripture shows the Roman soldiers stripped Jesus not once, but thrice. At first they took off His own clothes, leaving Him naked. This was before they put a scarlet robe on Him. When they had made jest of Him, they afterwards took off the scarlet robe, leaving Him naked the second time, before putting His own robe on Him. At Golgotha, before they crucified Him on the cross, they took off His clothes again, stripping Him for the third time.

In order to compound the mental and emotional torture, they parted His garment into four, divided it among themselves, and cast lot with dice for His coat before His very eyes. What a barbaric acts against an innocent and harmless man, who for grace's sake took our guilt and shame upon Himself. All these maltreatments He endured knowing that His nakedness meant our covering. There He was the holy Son of God hanged naked on the cross. What a sight of shame it might have seemed to all the onlookers, but was the price for our glorification in Him.

The Price of Being Crowned with Thorns

"And when they had platted a crown of thorns, they put it upon his head, and a reed in his right hand: and they bowed the knee before him, and mocked him, saying, Hail, King of the Jews! And they spit upon him, and took the reed, and smote him on the head." **Matthew 27: 29-30.**

"And the soldiers platted a crown of thorns, and put it on his head, and they put on him a purple robe," **John 19:2**

Could you imagine the pain of a thorn nail stuck deep into your hand; you wouldn't have an ounce of peace until it was taken off. But with the Lord, that wasn't the case. It was not just a thorn stuck into His head, but a crown of thorns with the multiple thorn nails sticking out all around the crown. They did not just place the crown of thorns on His head, but pressed it deep into His head, which caused blood to drip all over His face. Worst of all, they took the staff they had placed on His hand and struck His head with it, while the crown of thorns was still in His head. Imagine the excruciating pains. All their acts of injustice against Him are tantamount to devilish tortures. The crown of thorns they placed on Him actually was God putting all the curses of the Law that was due us on Him.

The Price of False Accusations

"Now the chief priests, and elders, and all the council, sought false witness against Jesus, to put him to death; But found none: yea, though many false witnesses came, yet found they none. At the last came two false witnesses, And said, This fellow said, I am able to

destroy the temple of God, and to build it in three days. And the high priest arose, and said unto him, Answerest thou nothing? what is it which these witness against thee?" **Matthew 26:59-62.**

"And the chief priests and all the council sought for witness against Jesus to put him to death; and found none. For many bare false witness against him, but their witness agreed not together. And there arose certain, and bare false witness against him, saying, We heard him say, I will destroy this temple that is made with hands, and within three days I will build another made without hands. But neither so did their witness agree together. And the high priest stood up in the midst, and asked Jesus, saying, Answerest thou nothing? what is it which these witness against thee? But

he held his peace, and answered nothing. Again the high priest asked him, and said unto him, Art thou the Christ, the Son of the Blessed?" **Mark 14:55-61.**

"And the whole multitude of them arose, and led him unto Pilate. And they began to accuse him, saying, We found this fellow perverting the nation, and forbidding to give tribute to Caesar, saying that he himself is Christ a King. And Pilate asked him, saying, Art thou the King of the Jews? And he answered him and said, Thou sayest it. Then said Pilate to the chief priests and to the people, I find no fault in this man. And they were the more fierce, saying, He stirreth up the people, teaching throughout all Jewry, beginning from Galilee to this place." **Luke 23:1-5**

A common enemy, most of the time, really has a

way of unifying vicious opposing rivals into an evil alliance. So was the case with the chief priest and elders and all the council, as they sought false witness against Jesus to put Him to death. But they found none, though many witnesses came forward to testify. Due to their strong conspiracy to get rid of Him, they kept up the enquiry, though the continual false witnesses and testimony against Him did not agree. Afterwards, two witnesses came forward and accused Him of saying He will destroy the temple and build it in three days. Was that really a crime punishable by death? Of course not!

Finally, the high priest charged Him by the living God to tell them if He was the Messiah; when He rightly answered yes, then they shouted blasphemy! 'He deserve to die', for what? Is it for telling the truth? The irony of the matter was that they were the one committing blasphemy against Him, because He was the Messiah as He claimed. Hence, their charge of blasphemy against Him was totally a false accusation.

THE COST

To compound their hypocrisies and double standards, they falsified a different allegation against Him before Pilate, in order to make Pilate buy into their evil cause: they deceitfully switched the brush from religious to political. They painted Christ as citing a rebellion against Rome or Caesar's authority, but Pilate saw through their whims and refused to buy it. He knew that their conspiracy and allegations against Jesus were based on envy. Nonetheless, they subtly succeeded in pushing Pilate into a tight corner, alleging that he is no friend of Caesar if he set Christ free.

All these incidents, mishap as they seem, had to take place for the scripture to be fulfilled concerning Him. Therefore, the cost of grace was His death. He had to die for humanity to access grace for salvation. God, who works all things after the counsel of His will, was obviously working behind the scene to accomplish His eternal purpose, foreordained in Christ before the foundation of the world. Christ was wrongly accused and suffered false allegation, in order that He might free us from the accuser of the brethren, Satan, and rid us of all satanic accusations.

The Price of False Labels

"Then answered the Jews, and said unto him, Say we not well that thou art a Samaritan, and hast a devil?" **John 8:48**

"Saying, Sir, we remember that that deceiver said, while he was yet alive, After three days I will rise again." **Matthew 27:63**

"And many of them said, He hath a devil, and is mad; why hear ye him? Others said, These are not the words of him that hath a devil. Can a devil open the eyes of the blind?" **John 10:20-21**

Most of us are quite aware of the shame and pain of being stigmatized. It may be bearable when a criminal is being stigmatized, for the crime committed and the just retribution of being imprisoned and labelled as 'ex-convict'. Nonetheless, it's unbearable when an innocent man is unjustly labelled a criminal. Such was the case of the sinless Son of God. Although He was the embodiment of truth and came to testify of truth, for envy, they labelled Him a deceiver.

In John 8:48, they labelled Him as a Samaritan and one under the power of a demon. How could they have come to these conclusions on someone they hadn't caught red-handed with the crime they accused Him of? It's nothing else but the slander of Satan; that is a part of the price Christ needed to pay for our redemption. They labelled Him not even as a Good Samaritan but one possessed with an evil spirit. A Samaritan is considered by the Jews as a contaminated and corrupted mixed race of Israel; they consider them idolaters and want no dealings with them. When they called Christ a Samaritan, they were implying that He was an outsider, an outcast, unholy and impure who they wanted no dealing with.

Likewise in John 10:20, the opposing Jews labelled Him mad and demonic; such labels are unwitting blasphemy. Regardless of their motives or state of ignorance, to label or stigmatize the Perfect One as mad is patently absurd. It's no wonder the Lord on the cross said, Father forgive them, for they do not have a clue of what they are doing. All these humiliations of our Lord are the high cost of grace.

The Price of (humiliation of the cross) Being Reviled

"And set up over his head his accusation written, THIS IS JESUS THE KING OF THE JEWS. Then were there two thieves crucified with him, one on the right hand, and another on the left. And they that passed by reviled him, wagging their heads, And saying, Thou that destroyest the temple, and buildest it in three days, save thyself. If thou be the Son of God, come down from the cross. Likewise also the chief

THE COST

priests mocking him, with the scribes and elders, said, He saved others; himself he cannot save. If he be the King of Israel, let him now come down from the cross, and we will believe him. He trusted in God; let him deliver him now, if he will have him: for he said, I am the Son of God. The thieves also, which were crucified with him, cast the same in his teeth." **Matthew 27:39-44**

"Let Christ the King of Israel descend now from the cross, that we may see and believe. And they that were crucified with him reviled him." **Mark 15:32**

"Who, when he was reviled, reviled not again; when he suffered, he threatened not; but committed himself to him that judgeth righteously:" **1 Peter 2:23**

To revile is to defame, rail at, chide, taunt, upbraid,

and reproach. After the Lord Jesus had been brutally beaten and battered beyond recognition by the cruel Roman soldiers, under the watchful eyes of His envious and false accusers, He was made to carry His cross (see John 19:17) as a common criminal. He was being led to Golgotha, as a lamb to the slaughter, to be crucified. So weakened and fainted, by reason of the merciless scourging (Matthew 27: 32), Simon of Cyrene was compelled to help Him bear the cross.

At Golgotha, He was nailed to the cross as depicted in the movie 'The Passion of the Christ'. He was not tied to the cross, as some other movies depicted, but was nailed hands and feet to the cross. The spikes actually went through His hands and feet. The nail holes still exist in His hands up till date. To these nail holes, Thomas alluded, unless he sees them he would not believe. Later, when the Master appeared, He said, Thomas, reach out and put your finger and behold my hands – which shows that the holes where evident in His hands and feet and still are.

THE COST

There He was, the spotless Son of God, who was for sinner slain, hanged on a cross amongst two thieves, in fulfilment of the scripture that said, 'He was numbered with the wicked'. Could you imagine the pain of the nail spikes? Even more dreadful is the excruciating pain, as a result of His whole weight being held up on the cross by the spikes. Oh what He must have felt and thought hanging there. What a great price to pay for our sins. As someone rightly exclaimed, it wasn't the nail that held Him on the Cross, but our sins.

These pains would have been more than enough price to pay for grace. Notwithstanding, in addition to the agonizing pain, the Jews, their then-blind leaders, the Roman soldiers, the thief and the passersby yet reviled Him. They railed at Him, they upbraided Him, some taunted Him, and others defamed and reproached Him waging their head. The worst of it all was not just the inhumane words they used on Him, but how sardonically they said it.

"And those who passed by kept reviling

Him and reproaching Him abusively in harsh and insolent language, wagging their heads and saying, Aha! You Who would destroy the temple and build it in three days, Now rescue Yourself [from death], coming down from the cross! So also the chief priests, with the scribes, made sport of Him to one another, saying, He rescued others [from death]; Himself He is unable to rescue. Let the Christ (the Messiah), the King of Israel, come down now from the cross, that we may see [it] and trust in and rely on Him and adhere to Him! Those who were crucified with Him also reviled and reproached Him [speaking abusively, harshly, and insolently]." **Mark 15:29-32 (Amplified)**

In Matthew 27:44 and in Luke 23:39-43 alike, we see one of the criminals who was also condemned to death joined in on the insult. The verse said: He railed on Jesus – implying he abused and insulted Christ with hash and insolent language. How low can He get? When a common criminal sees it fit to insult the righteous and Holy One of God; yet the Lord answered him not a word. The other criminal was the one who rebuked his rude mate; he also justified the Lord as Pilate did, stating that the Lord Jesus did not deserve the condemnation He had received (Luke 23:39-43).

His Cry of Agony on the Cross

"Now from the sixth hour there was darkness over all the land unto the ninth hour. And about the ninth hour Jesus cried with a loud voice, saying, Eli, Eli, lama sabachthani? that is to say, My God, my God, why hast thou forsaken me? Some of them that stood there, when they heard that, said, This man calleth for Elias. And straightway one of them ran, and took a spunge, and filled it with vinegar, and put it on a

reed, and gave him to drink. The rest said, Let be, let us see whether Elias will come to save him. Jesus, when he had cried again with a loud voice, yielded up the ghost." **Matthew 27:45-50**

"And when Jesus had cried with a loud voice, he said, Father, into thy hands I commend my spirit: and having said thus, he gave up the ghost." **Luke 23:46**

"After this, Jesus knowing that all things were now accomplished, that the scripture might be fulfilled, saith, I thirst. Now there was set a vessel full of vinegar: and they filled a spunge with vinegar, and put it upon hyssop, and put it to his mouth. When Jesus therefore had received the vinegar, he said, It is finished: and he bowed his head, and gave up the ghost." **John 19:28-30**

THE COST

No doubt, this must have been the deadliest punch of all dilemmas the Lord had to endure: to be separated from His Father, to the point He felt forsaken by Him. Of all the afflictions and betrays, being denied and forsaken by His most trusted friends, Christ never raised His voice, but when He felt left alone by His Father, He cried aloud in agony. The cruel strokes and mockery did not make Him cry, the excruciating pain from being nailed hands and feet to the cross did not make Him cry as loud. Why then, is He now crying this loud?

Could it be due to the fact that He had never been separated from His Beloved and Blessed Father in all His existence? Perhaps the very thought of such separation was what terrified Him in the garden of Gethsemane. Apparently; this agonizing cry of being separated or forsaken by the Father seems to suggest so. Oh! How glad we are that He did not come down from the cross as they taunted Him to. He was forsaken, so that we might be forgiven. He was rejected, so that we might be accepted. Obviously, of the entire cup and baptizing of suffering He drank, this for sure was the most bitter of all.

It's worth emphasizing that He was not forced or coerced into going through these passions on our behalf. Rather, He willingly chose to lay down His life as a ransom for our redemption. At the cry of an anguishing soul, He said, *"I thirst"*. Rather than give Him water, the soldiers gave Him vinegar. Nonetheless, the vinegar represents the bitter judgment of death He tested for all men (see Hebrew 2:9). For the grace of God, He indeed tasted death for us, which was the ultimate price for grace.

The Bible says in John 19:28 that Jesus, knowing in Himself that all things were now accomplished and that the scripture might be fulfilled, said: *"It is finished"*. And He bowed His head and gave up the ghost. He did not die until He had fulfilled all the prophecies of scripture concerning Him. He made sure He accomplished His redemptive mission to the letter, and then He declared it is finished, meaning the price is paid in full. Nothing more, nothing less, and nothing else; His death was a foreordained means of God to accomplish our salvation.

> *"And, having made peace through the blood of his cross, by him to reconcile all things unto himself; by him, I say, whether they be things in earth, or things in heaven. And you, that were sometime alienated and enemies in your mind by wicked works, yet now hath he reconciled In the body of his flesh through death, to present you holy and unblameable and unreproveable in his sight:"* **Colossians 1:20-22.**

His death indeed was a means. Obviously it was not a coincident that, immediately after He yielded up the ghost, the scripture said: "And behold, the veil of the temple was rent from top to bottom; and the earth did quake and the rock rent." Amazing! All this shaking and renting was a statement or a press released from heaven, stating that, henceforth, God is available and accessible by all through the grace of our Lord and Saviour Jesus Christ, who has offered Himself to buy our pardon and has tasted death for everyone.

> *"And they that passed by reviled him, wagging their heads, And saying, Thou that destroyest the temple, and buildest it in three days, save thyself. If thou be the Son of God, come down from the cross."* **Matthew 27:39-40**

The hub of all that the Lord's critics and mockers used against Him was His claimed identity; the propensity of all their attacks were really the core of who He said He is. Such acts on their part reflect the influences of the tempter upon them. They, like their master, the devil, were tempting Him to prove who He claimed to be. His core claims were that He is the Son of God, the Sent and Anointed One, the King of His Kingdom, the Bread of Life, etc. Evidently, for these claims He was despised, rejected, accused of blasphemy, tempted, tried and crucified.

In view of these whole incidents, a question comes to mind. Could it be that the object of Satan's attack on us is the core of who we are in Christ? Should that be the case, why so then? Do you suppose that who we are determines our response in life? Implying that, what we do and how we live our lives as children of God is a direct derivative of who we perceive ourselves to be? Definitely so! As a man thinks, so is he.

Opposition to His Resurrection

> *"Now the next day, that followed the day of the preparation, the chief priests and Pharisees came together unto Pilate, Saying, Sir, we remember that that deceiver said, while he was yet alive, After three days I will rise again. Command therefore that the sepulchre be made sure until the third day, lest his*

disciples come by night, and steal him away, and say unto the people, He is risen from the dead: so the last error shall be worse than the first. Pilate said unto them, Ye have a watch: go your way, make it as sure as ye can. So they went, and made the sepulchre sure, sealing the stone, and setting a watch."
Matthew 27: 62:-66

"And, behold, there was a great earthquake: for the angel of the Lord descended from heaven, and came and rolled back the stone from the door, and sat upon it. His countenance was like lightning, and his raiment white as snow: And for fear of him the keepers did shake, and became as dead men... Now when they were going, behold, some of the watch came into the city, and shewed unto the chief priests all the things that were done. And when they were assembled with the elders, and

THE COST

had taken counsel, they gave large money unto the soldiers, Saying, Say ye, His disciples came by night, and stole him away while we slept. And if this come to the governor's ears, we will persuade him, and secure you. So they took the money, and did as they were taught: and this saying is commonly reported among the Jews until this day." **Matthew 28: 2-4, 11-15**

One would think that after the Lord's death, His adversaries would relent, but they didn't. They went and requested permission from Pilate to secure the grave; which I see now as a God Idea. Had they not secured the grave, they would have been more persuaded to deny the resurrection of Christ. But with their set guards on guard, they had first-class witness of the resurrection of Christ. Although they in pretence denied the resurrection, it limited how far they would have gone to discredit the resurrection without those guards. Almost everything Christ is, stood for, and did, was met with oppositions in an attempt to frustrate His every effort, but He overcame every such resistance every time. They opposed His birth in an attempt to kill Him. They opposed His miraculous deeds, saying He did them by Beelzebub. They opposed His teachings, calling Him a false teacher. They opposed His death and they opposed His resurrection. Even now there is an opposition to His return; as they couldn't stop Him then, they can't stop Him now! Hallelujah!

The lessons to be leant here is that: if they opposed the Master, Perfect and Powerful as He was, it will be arrogance of the highest order for any saint or servant of God to expect to do anything good in life without demonic opposition. Especially when it comes to any form of Ministry or Divine Assignment, know for sure that it is spiritual warfare. One must also know for sure that He that sent us is with us, and that He is greater than he that is against us. This is our consolation and confidence: *"that they that be for us are more than they that are be against us."*

CHAPTER THREE
THE CAUSE

"Now our Lord Jesus Christ himself, and God, even our Father, which hath loved us, and hath given us everlasting consolation and good hope through grace, Comfort your hearts, and stablish you in every good word and work." **2 Thessalonians 2:16-17**

"And the LORD God of their fathers sent to them by his messengers, rising up betimes, and sending; because he had compassion on his people, and on his dwelling place: But they mocked the messengers of God, and despised his words, and misused his prophets, until

THE COST OF GRACE

the wrath of the LORD arose against his people, till there was no remedy." **2 Chronicles 36:15-16**

The word 'cause' is defined as a person or thing that gives rise to an action, phenomena, or condition. It is also a reason to feel something or to behave a particular way; a producer of an effect; a reason or motive for some human action or condition. In view of these various definitions of the word 'CAUSE', the cause of grace then is what gave rise to the condition of grace. It is the reason or motive behind the benevolent acts of the God of all grace, to make grace available and accessible to all humans.

The ultimate question to be answered here is: why would God even care, or go through that much, to pay such an unfathomable and incalculable high price to save mankind by His grace? We are not alone in this question. A great king of Israel, David, asked the same question in Psalm 8:3-4:

"When I consider thy heavens, the work

> *of thy fingers, the moon and the stars, which thou hast ordained; What is man, that thou art mindful of him? and the son of man, that thou visitest him?"*

In a sense, King David was asking God: why do you care so meticulously as you do for man; do they really deserve it? Thank God, for giving us the answer through the mouth of His only Begotten Son, our Lord and Saviour Jesus Christ. In His conversation with Nicodemus, the Lord unveiled the motivating factor behind all the Godhead actions to humanity – which is LOVE. Yes! That is the CAUSE: LOVE! It is the motivating factor behind all of God's actions to mankind. LOVE is the CAUSE of GRACE.

> *"For God so loved the world, that he gave his only begotten Son, that whosoever believeth in him should not perish, but have everlasting life."* **John 3:16**

This most popular verse of the Bible is self-explanatory. Reason being: it is the summary of the whole Bible. God had to be sure the capsule of the gospel message was uncomplicated; unambiguously simple to swallow; easy to memorise; sweet to quote, and yet powerful. It simply shows that the reason why God sent His Son is because He LOVES us. Love was the reason for Creation, Redemption, and future Restitution. The problem was sin. The remedy was Salvation. Salvation could only be available by grace. Motivated by Love, God sent Jesus Christ to pay the ultimate price to make grace that brings Salvation available to all.

> *"Therefore doth my Father love me, because I lay down my life, that I might take it again. No man taketh it from me, but I lay it down of myself. I have power to lay it down, and I have power to take it again. This commandment have I received of my Father."* **John 10:17-18**

THE CAUSE

"Greater love hath no man than this, that a man lay down his life for his friends." **John 15:13.**

"Now before the feast of the passover, when Jesus knew that his hour was come that he should depart out of this world unto the Father, having loved his own which were in the world, he loved them unto the end." **John 13:1**

The implication of this verse is that: the Lord loves us wholeheartedly, and because He did, He willingly laid His life down according to His Father's will and gladly became our ransom. In Christ, priestly prayer for us His Church in John 17:19. He made a profound statement, that 'for our sake He had sanctified Himself' so that we also might be sanctified through Him. In other words, because Jesus loves us, He presented and dedicated Himself to God as the required and needed perfect sacrifice for our sins.

THE COST OF GRACE

Clear Prove of God's Love

"And hope maketh not ashamed; because the love of God is shed abroad in our hearts by the Holy Ghost which is given unto us. For when we were yet without strength, in due time Christ died for the ungodly. For scarcely for a righteous man will one die: yet peradventure for a good man some would even dare to die. But God commendeth his love toward us, in that, while we were yet sinners, Christ died for us. Much more then, being now justified by his blood, we shall be saved from wrath through him. For if, when we were enemies, we were reconciled to God by the death of his Son, much more, being reconciled, we shall be saved by his life. And not only so, but we also joy in God through our Lord Jesus Christ, by whom we have

THE CAUSE

now received the atonement."
Romans 5:5-11

This passage of scripture is clear proof of God's motivating factor: LOVE! On the other hand, it is a clear dismissal of any demoralizing doubt that may arise to question the validity of God's love for us. Here are the impregnable and irrefutable evidences.

The Holy writ asserts that, while we were yet in weakness, powerless to help ourselves out of the misery of sin and its consequence of deaths and damnations, Christ – for love's sake – died for us in our ungodly state. Wow! Thank you, Jesus!

Irrefutable evidence two: Apostle Paul argued that it would be an extraordinary occurrence for anyone to give his or her life for a righteous man. Perhaps for a notable, loveable, and extremely generous benefactor, someone might even dare to die. But in order for God to prove beyond doubt how much He loved us, while we were still living in sins as sinners, Christ came and died for us. As a result of that gracious act of love, we have been justified by His blood and shall be saved from God's wrath through Him.

Irrefutable evidence number three: verse ten of Romans 5 says, we were God's enemies when Christ died on our behalf to reconcile us to God. Then, the question becomes: what would make one die for his enemies? Nothing else but Agape-love, which is the God kind of love as demonstrated in the above passage of scripture. Hence, it is evidential that the CAUSE OF GRACE is the loving kindness and tender mercies of our Great God of Love.

For His Great Love

"But God, who is rich in mercy, for his great love wherewith he loved us, Even when we were dead in sins, hath quickened us together with Christ, (by grace ye are saved;) And hath raised us up together, and made us sit together in heavenly places in Christ Jesus: That in the ages to come he might shew the

exceeding riches of his grace in his kindness toward us through Christ Jesus." **Ephesians 2:4-7**

Apostle Paul began this chapter by reminding the saint: God has made them alive, who were once dead in sins and under the influence of Satan, and therefore, were children of wrath by nature. Then in verse four, he reminded them what alters their state of being and why. In other words, Paul is giving us the reason or motive behind God's action. He started the verse with "But God"; this is one of those divine 'buts' of the scriptures, which usually highlight God's divine and miraculous intervention in the lives of those who trust in Him. I heard a minister defined 'but' as zero: meaning a total negation or alteration of what previously is, or said, or done.

I hereby declare, as a servant of the Lord Jesus Christ, that any negative 'but' in the life of any dear reader be neutralized and negated in the glorious name of Jesus. Amen!

Let's look at the next phrase in verse four, which states: *"who is rich in mercy"*. Our God is exceedingly and extremely rich in His mercy, oh yes! His steadfast love never ceases and His mercies never come to an end. As a matter of fact, His mercies are new every morning. Imagine six thousand plus years of history, with six billion plus of humanity on planet Earth. His mercies have been available that long and that much, every morning to wake us all up each day! How rich is such mercy? It must be incalculable and immeasurable.

God's mercies are an outflow of His love. Furthermore, the next phrase says: *"for His great love where with He loved us"*. Let's examine the word 'for'. The word 'for' here simply means 'because,' which suggests the motivating factor behind the stated actions. In this case, it is clearly specified that it was because of His great love with which He loved us that made Him move in compassion to save us by grace. Therefore, it is evident that the cause of grace is due to His great love with which He loved us. The Amplified version renders it more explicitly: that it was because of, and in order to satisfy, the great and wonderful and intense love with which He loved us that He saved us by His grace.

He Gave Himself for Love

"I am crucified with Christ: nevertheless I live; yet not I, but Christ liveth in me: and the life which I now live in the flesh I live by the faith of the Son of God, who loved me, and gave himself for me."
Galatians 2:20

Apostle Paul's point of discussion in this verse is that Christ is our representational substitute; which means that Christ represented all humanity in His death. He that knew no sin died in our place who are sinners; He in that sense became our substitute, as the scapegoats offered under the Old Covenant became the substitute of those who offered them. The Apostle is emphasizing here that because Christ was crucified for him, he also has been crucified with Christ. As a result, his life is no longer his, but for the one who died for him. In other words, he, Paul, has ceased to exist, so that the life of Christ may be fully lived and expressed through his vessel. The underline truth to be drawn here is: Christ gave Himself for us. Paul's drawn conclusion, conviction, and confession is that because Christ loved him, He gave Himself for him. This is not only true for the Apostle but for you and me. It was for love that He gave Himself for us.

Here is His Love

"He that loveth not knoweth not God; for God is love. In this was manifested the love of God toward us, because that God sent his only begotten Son into the world, that we might live through him. Herein is love, not that we loved God, but that he loved us, and sent his Son to be the propitiation for our sins. Beloved, if God so loved us, we ought also to love

THE CAUSE

one another. We love him, because he first loved us." **1 John 4:8-11, 19**

Note the expression *'God is Love'*. He is not suggesting that God has love, but that He is love Himself. Consequently, because God is love, every one of His actions is love-based and motivated by love. Every benevolent act of our Father—God – is issued out of His love for His beloved creatures, made in His own image. Verse nine vividly declares that the height of the manifestation or display of God's love is the sending of His only begotten Son into the world to die for our sins, in order that we might live through Him. Verse ten also vividly portrays what love is truly all about: it exclaimed *"herein is love"*. He is simply saying: make no mistakes about it, just in case you aren't sure what love is, this is it. God did not send His Son because we love Him; no, not at all! Rather, He sent His Son to be our propitiation for our sins because He loves us.

The word propitiation simply means 'atoning

sacrifice'; it is a word that describes the sacrificial blood that the Levitical priest carries into the holy of holies to be placed on the mercy seat. The word is used interchangeably for mercy seat, which symbolizes Christ as our mercy seat. In a nut shell, it wasn't our love for God that prompted or motivated Him to save us from our misery of sin, but His unconditional and unfailing love for us. We only love Him because He first loved us.

> *"Be ye therefore followers of God, as dear children; And walk in love, as Christ also hath loved us, and hath given himself for us an offering and a sacrifice to God for a sweetsmelling savour."* **Ephesians 5:1-2**

We are being admonished here to be imitators of our heavenly Father, to copy and follow His examples as well-beloved children imitate their father. Our first step of imitation is to walk in sacrificial love, in the footsteps of Christ, who for love's sake gave Himself up as a slain offering and sacrifice to God for us. The understandable reason He gave Himself as the price for our ransom is because He loves us.

> *"Now our Lord Jesus Christ himself, and God, even our Father, which hath loved us, and hath given us everlasting consolation and good hope through grace, Comfort your hearts, and stablish you in every good word and work."* **2 Thessalonians 2:16-17**

> *"And from Jesus Christ, who is the faithful witness, and the first begotten of the dead, and the prince of the kings of the earth. Unto him that loved us, and washed us from our sins in his own blood, And hath made us kings and priests unto God and his Father; to him be glory and dominion for ever and ever. Amen."* **Revelation 1:5-6**

In these glorious verses, we see in plain sight who our Beloved Redeemer is; what He has done for us;

why He did it; and the effect of His blessed act of mercy. He is the Faithful Witness; the Perfect Representation of the Father: who only has seen the Father and faithfully and fearlessly made the Father known to us. He is the first begotten from the dead; the first-fruit of all creation: who was delivered for our offences and was raised again from the dead for our justification.

Jesus Christ is the Prince of the Kings of the earth; the King of kings and the Lord of lords; who rules all rulers, and rules in the affairs of men. This is He, who ever loved us, and because He ever loved us—has washed us from our sins by His own blood. Wow! The Amplified version renders the word 'washed' as 'loosed' and 'freed'; which indicates that Christ by His very own blood has loosed and freed us from ours.

We that were tangled up by sin, Christ has untangled by His own blood. We that were once bound up by the yoke of sin have been freed from the grip of sin by Christ's own blood, all because He loves us! Glory to God! Moreover, being washed from our sins, He has made us kings and priests unto His God and Father. To Him indeed belongs all the glory and dominion forever and ever, amen! What kind of love is this? It is certainly beyond human description; it is too marvellous for words and too wonderful for comprehension; this is God's love like an ocean. Hallelujah!

> *"What shall we then say to these things? If God be for us, who can be against us? He that spared not his own Son, but delivered him up for us all, how shall he not with him also freely give us all things? Who shall lay any thing to the charge of God's elect? It is God that justifieth. Who is he that condemneth? It is Christ that died, yea rather, that is risen again, who is even at the right hand of God, who also maketh intercession for us. Who shall separate us from the love of Christ? shall tribulation, or distress, or persecution,*

or famine, or nakedness, or peril, or sword? As it is written, For thy sake we are killed all the day long; we are accounted as sheep for the slaughter. Nay, in all these things we are more than conquerors through him that loved us. For I am persuaded, that neither death, nor life, nor angels, nor principalities, nor powers, nor things present, nor things to come, Nor height, nor depth, nor any other creature, shall be able to separate us from the love of God, which is in Christ Jesus our Lord."
Romans 8:31-39

"Because thy loving kindness is better than life, my lips shall praise thee."
Psalm 63:3

CHAPTER FOUR
THE EFFECT

"But after that the kindness and love of God our Saviour toward man appeared, Not by works of righteousness which we have done, but according to his mercy he saved us, by the washing of regeneration, and renewing of the Holy Ghost; Which he shed on us abundantly through Jesus Christ our Saviour; That being justified by his grace, we should be made heirs according to the hope of eternal life." **Titus 3:4-7**

"And now for a little space grace hath been shewed from the LORD our God, to leave us a remnant to escape, and to

give us a nail in his holy place, that our God may lighten our eyes, and give us a little reviving in our bondage." **Ezra 9:8**

In Acts 11:23, Barnabas was sent of the elders in Jerusalem to the new believers in Antioch. The scripture said, when he arrived and saw the grace of God, he was glad. What exactly did he see? A pile of grace? Certainly not! What he saw was the effect of grace. A people so transformed by the power of grace to reflect Christ, to the extent they were there named Christians.

> *"For the grace of God that bringeth salvation hath appeared to all men,"* **Titus 2:11**

The word 'effect' is defined as a change, which is a result or consequence of an action or other cause. Therefore, by 'effect of grace' I mean: the change in human state which is a result or consequence of the grace of our Lord Jesus Christ. In the gospel according to Saint John, Apostle John unveiled to us in chapter one, verse sixteen and seventeen, that

THE EFFECT

of Christ's fullness, we have all received grace upon grace. And that the Law was given by Moses, but grace and truth came by Jesus Christ. What needs to be noted here are two underlined factors:

#1: That grace has come.

#2: That it came through Jesus Christ.

With that in mind, let us see what Titus has to say about the effect of grace: Titus 2:11, above, affirmed and confirmed that grace has actually appeared unto all men, but not empty handed. Rather more importantly, grace brought salvation with Him. The obvious conclusion then is that the effect of grace is SALVATION.

> *"Even when we were dead in sins, hath quickened us together with Christ, (by grace ye are saved;)... For by grace are ye saved through faith; and that not of yourselves: it is the gift of God: Not of works, lest any man should boast."*
> **Ephesians 2:5,8-9**

What is salvation? To begin with, let's look at it from the Old Testament perspective. The Hebrew word translated to 'salvation' in the Old Testament is 'yeshuwah', which means deliverance. The first occurrence is in Jacob's last words in Geneses 49:18, which says, *"I have waited for thy salvation, O Lord"*. Salvation in the Old Testament is not understood as salvation from sin, since the word denotes broadly anything from which deliverance must be sought, such as; distress, war, servitude or enemies.

In view of that, salvation is understood by the Old Testament saint as aid, help, health, welfare, victory, rescued, preserved prosperity, and safety. Although there are divine and human deliverers, deliverance is thus generally used with God as the subject. God is known as the salvation of His people (see Deuteronomy 32:15, Isaiah 12:2). The wonders He worked on behalf of His people are His salvation (Psalm 98:1).

Under the New Testament, the word 'salvation' in the

THE EFFECT

Greek language is used in a variety of ways. In one sense, it corresponds with the Old Testament Hebrew word '*yeshuwah*'. The Greek word is '*sozo*', which denote to save, deliver, or protect; it also means to be made whole, to heal, preserve, do well, safe or rescue. '*Sozo*', which denote *"to save"*, is used with the noun '*soteria*', which denotes *"salvation"* – meaning deliverance or preservation. Hence, salvation is used in the New Testament as material or temporal deliverance from danger and apprehension, such as national or personal deliverance, either from the sea, prison, flood, or sickness.

Beyond that, salvation is mainly used in the New Testament of the spiritual and eternal deliverance granted immediately by God to those who accept His conditions of repentance and faith in the Lord Jesus, in whom alone it is to be obtained (Acts 4:12), and upon confession of Jesus Christ as Lord (Romans 10:10), for this purpose the gospel is the saving instrument (Romans 1:16). Salvation is also used for the present experience of God's power to deliver from the bondage of sin. Salvation is also used for the future deliverance of believers at the return of Christ for His saints, which is the object of our confident hope of being delivered from the wrath of God destined to be executed upon the ungodly at the end of this age (1 Thessalonians 1:10).

Salvation is also used for the deliverance of the nation of Israel at the second coming of Christ at the time of His appearance (Revelation 12:10). More also, salvation is used inclusively to sum up all the blessings bestowed by God on men in Christ through the Holy Spirit (2 Corinthians 6:2 / 1 Peter 1:9-10).

The point to be made, regardless of the Old Testament and New Testament perspectives or concepts of salvation, is that: salvation in any sense is a work of God's grace. Therefore, the EFFECT OF GRACE IS SALVATION. And salvation is deliverance from sin and its consequences, and the possession of ETERNAL LIFE with all of God's blessings or riches through the sacrificial death, burial, resurrection, ascension, and exaltation of our Lord and saviour Jesus Christ.

The true essence of salvation is intimacy with God, for now and eternity. The effect of grace is salvation and the effect of salvation is intimacy with God that leads to heartfelt service for Him.

Components of Salvation

"But, beloved, we are persuaded better things of you, and things that accompany salvation, though we thus speak." **Hebrew 6:9**

The word salvation is a compound word with various components that encapsulate the totality of what God in Christ has wrought for mankind. In order to have a thorough understanding of the word salvation, it would be wise to take the components apart momentary for the sake of detail and specific examination, before coupling them back again. Such components of salvation include: justification, redemption, righteousness, sanctification, divine life and nature, blessings, hope, prosperity, security and preservation, etc.

> *"Bless the LORD, O my soul: and all that is within me, bless his holy name. Bless the LORD, O my soul, and forget not all his benefits: Who forgiveth all thine iniquities; who healeth all thy diseases; Who redeemeth thy life from destruction; who crowneth thee with lovingkindness and tender mercies; Who satisfieth thy mouth with good things; so that thy youth is renewed like the eagle's. The LORD executeth righteousness and judgment for all that are oppressed." Psalm 103:1-6*

> *"But of him are ye in Christ Jesus, who of God is made unto us wisdom, and righteousness, and sanctification, and redemption:"* **1 Corinthians 1:30**

THE EFFECT

Justifies Freely by Grace

"Being justified freely by his grace through the redemption that is in Christ Jesus:" **Romans 3:24**

"That being justified by his grace, we should be made heirs according to the hope of eternal life." **Titus 3:7**

In accordance with these verses, justification is an effect or consequence of grace. It is as a result of the grace of God that men are justified. Justification or to be justified means to be declared innocent of guilt; it's to be pronounced righteous and be shown to be right. In other words, justification is the legal and former acquittal from guilt by God as judge, the pronouncement of the sinner as righteous who believes on the Lord Jesus Christ. Justification is the gift of no condemnation to those that are in Christ (Romans 8:1).

Ideally, the complete fulfilment of the Law of God would provide a basis of justification for such a one in the sight of God. Unfortunately, no such case has occurred in mere human experience, and therefore, no one can be justified by the Law in the sight of God. But thank God that, consistent with His righteous character as the Just and Justifier, He has through the grace of Christ made full and complete provision for the justification of all who would put their faith in Jesus' blood. Titus 3:7 not only affirmed that we are justified by His grace, but also confirmed that we have been made heirs according to the hope of eternal life. It is by the grace of God that we have inherited eternal life.

Reigning In Life

> "But not as the offence, so also is the free gift. For if through the offence of one many be dead, much more the grace of God, and the gift by grace, which is by one man, Jesus Christ, hath abounded unto many. And not as it was by one that sinned, so is the gift: for the judgment was by one to condemnation, but the free gift is of

THE EFFECT

many offences unto justification. For if by one man's offence death reigned by one; much more they which receive abundance of grace and of the gift of righteousness shall reign in life by one, Jesus Christ.)... That as sin hath reigned unto death, even so might grace reign through righteousness unto eternal life by Jesus Christ our Lord."
Romans 5:15-17, 21

In this passage of scripture, the writer is comparing the entrance, medium, and the effect of sin into and on the human race with the entrance, medium, and effect of grace into and on the human race. His drawn conclusion is that sin came into the world through Adam's disobedience, which resulted in the death of all humans. Nonetheless, in contrast to Adam, Christ through His obedience has made grace available and accessible to all mankind, which has resulted as a free gift of righteousness to reign in life. He stresses the fact that the payment of grace by Christ far supersedes the effect of sin. The Lord did not just pay the debt of sins we owned, but overpaid them in the fullest term possible.

Those of us that have put our faith in the Lord Jesus have received the abundance of grace and the gift of righteousness to reign in life. Hence, the main key for reigning in life is the grace of Christ. The effect of grace therefore includes the free gift of righteousness and the power to reign as kings in life. May the grace of our blessed God abound onto us to reign as king in life, in Jesus' glorious name!

Safe Standing

> *"Therefore being justified by faith, we have peace with God through our Lord Jesus Christ: By whom also we have access by faith into this grace wherein we stand, and rejoice in hope of the glory of God."* **Romans 5:1-2**

Although grace is what really justified us, faith is how our justification is appropriated. Grace paid for it, but faith is the hand that receives it. And as a result

THE EFFECT

of our justification, we now have and enjoy the peace of reconciliation with our heavenly Father. Oh what a blessing of grace! Verse two made it clear that it is due to our faith in the Lord Jesus Christ that we now have access into God's grace "wherein we stand". Note the phrase "wherein we stand"; this simply implies that we are standing safely in grace. One may be wondering what it means to be standing in grace; it simply means we are standing in the state of God's favour.

The word translated as 'stand' here also means to be stabled, appointed, abide, and hold up. Standing in grace means we are established in God's unmerited favour; we have been appointed to God's unmerited favour; we have been made to abide in God's unmerited favour; and we are been held up by God's unmerited favour. Not only are we standing in grace, but we have also been position under grace. As a result, we have grace under our feet to hold us up and grace above us to shield us down, for the Word declares that we are under grace.

"For sin shall not have dominion over you: for ye are not under the law, but under grace. What then? Shall we sin, because we are not under the law, but under grace? God forbid." **Romans 6:14-15**

God's Elect

"Even so then at this present time also there is a remnant according to the election of grace. And if by grace, then is it no more of works: otherwise grace is no more grace. But if it be of works, then is it no more grace: otherwise work is no more work." **Romans 11:5-6**

The scriptures in Colossians 3:12 refer to us as "the elect of God, holy and beloved". What a blessed title? This is as good as it gets – to be God's elect, holy and beloved. Awesome! This is the gospel truth of what grace has made us. The Apostle in the above verse is reminding the Saints of how that blessed title of being God's elect was conferred on them, which is by means of grace alone. Hence, our election is only by the grace of God.

What Makes A Man

"But by the grace of God I am what I am: and his grace which was bestowed upon me was not in vain; but I laboured more abundantly than they all: yet not I, but the grace of God which was with me." **1 Corinthians 15:10**

One of my pastor friends came to our men's conference a year ago and preached a message titled, *"It's God That Makes a Man"*. How true! Meanwhile, God makes a man by means of His grace. Thus, we can as well say that it's grace that makes a man. He was right on the money; it is the exact same truth Apostle Paul emphasized in the verse above. He said it's by the grace of God that he has attained what he has attained in Christ and has achieved what he has achieved in life. He further emphasized that the grace he received was not fruitless and without effect, but by it he laboured abundantly above all the other Apostles. He then consented and concluded that, although he had laboured earnestly, the credit for such effort is not his, but credited to the grace of God.

This truth right here has made void all human boasting and any fleshly reasons for being puffed up. It is only by grace that Godly men are made. Like one of our sisters use to say: none of us is an achiever, we are all receivers. This is in line with the scriptural verses which say: what have you that you have not received? Everything we have is truly by the mercies and grace of God, period! It's by grace we are saved and called, and it is by grace we fulfil our calling. I am reminded of the chorus: *"Only by grace can we enter, only by grace can we stand, not by our human endeavour but by the blood of the Lamb."*

"But when it pleased God, who

separated me from my mother's womb, and called me by his grace," **Galatians 1:15**

"Whereof I was made a minister, according to the gift of the grace of God given unto me by the effectual working of his power." **Ephesians 3:7**

All Sufficiency

"And God is able to make all grace abound toward you; that ye, always having all sufficiency in all things, may abound to every good work:" **2 Corinthians 9:8**

The word of the Lord has admonished us not to be a sparing sower but a generous one; that as we do well to give generously and cheerfully, God – who loves a cheerful giver – will make all grace abound towards us. The effect of God's abounding grace would be all suffering in all things. Generous and cheerful giving does not only open doors for earthly blessings, but opens heavenly windows for spiritual blessings also. More also, it is a great ripple effect or chain reaction as verse nine to fifteen explains. As we are obedient to sow the seeds God gives us, our seeds then become bread for others, and as a result, God multiplies our seeds back to us as harvest and increases our fruit of righteousness. As those we help are also able to help others, it continues in a circle and abounds in thanksgiving unto God by everyone who is affected by our faithfulness and commitment to the gospel.

Redemption

> *"In whom we have redemption through his blood, the forgiveness of sins, according to the riches of his grace;"*
> **Ephesians 1:7**

It is in Christ alone that humanity is guaranteed redemption. There is no other way or source of redemption except in the precious blood of Jesus Christ. The word translated as 'redemption' here is the Greek word 'apolutrosis'; this word means to be purchased from the slave market of sin, totally set free, never to be sold again. It is use here in Ephesians 1:7 as forgiveness of sins, indicating both the liberation from the guilt and doom of sin and the introduction into a life of liberty with newness of life.

The excitement of this wonderful redemption is that: it is in accordance to the riches of God's grace. In other words, our redemption was due to God's riches at the expense of Christ. Our God is truly rich in grace. He has, in accordance with the riches and the generosity of His gracious favour, purchased us from the slave market of sin, by the precious blood of His son. He has totally set us free, never to be sold again. This is amazing grace!

This benevolent act of love is the partial fulfilment of God's ongoing plan to clearly demonstrate through the ages to come the immeasurable riches of His free grace in His kindness and goodness of heart towards us in Christ Jesus (see Ephesians 2:7 Amplified).

Everlasting Consolation and Good Hope

"Now our Lord Jesus Christ himself, and God, even our Father, which hath loved us, and hath given us everlasting consolation and good hope through grace, Comfort your hearts, and stablish you in every good word and work." **2 Thessalonians 2:16-17**

Hidden in this intermediary benediction of Paul the Apostle to the Thessalonians Church are clusters of a sum total of the effects of grace. The breakdown of these clusters is that: because the Father and the Lord Jesus Christ loved us, they have given us everlasting consolation and good hope through grace. Note that what He has given is not just temporary consolation, but everlasting consolation. Note also that the hope given is not just mere hope, but good hope. All this conferred blessedness came to us by no other means, but by means of grace. Hallelujah!

What then is this everlasting consolation and good

hope? I am convinced that it is a sum total of all that the Father has wrought for us in the redemptive work of grace through Jesus Christ. Simply put, it is the total package of salvation we have received by grace through faith in our Lord and Saviour Jesus Christ. That same truth is echoed as well by Apostle Paul in 2 Timothy 1:9, which states that God has saved us and called us to a holy life, not because of anything we have done, but because of His own purpose and grace. All these truths clearly show that our Salvation, calling, and all manifested purposes of God concerning us are totally the effect of His grace.

No More Taste of Death

> *"But we see Jesus, who was made a little lower than the angels for the suffering of death, crowned with glory and honour; that he by the grace of God should taste death for every man. For it became him, for whom are all things, and by whom are all things, in bringing*

many sons unto glory, to make the captain of their salvation perfect through sufferings. For both he that sanctifieth and they who are sanctified are all of one: for which cause he is not ashamed to call them brethren,"
Hebrew 2:9-11

The glorious juices of these verses of scripture are that our Glorious High God was made lower than the angels, for a little while, in order that He, by the grace of God, should taste death for every man. In other words, the Lord Jesus Christ – for whom are all things and from whom are all things – died to experience death for every individual person. And because He tasted death for us by His grace, we are not to taste or experience death any longer. This is what He meant in John 11:26 when He said: *"whosoever liveth and believeth in me shall never die"*.

And because He died our death spiritually, we that are in Him shall die no more spiritually. He, by the

Grace of God, was delivered up for our offenses and has been raised again for our justification. There is, therefore, no condemnation to us that are in Christ Jesus. For the law of the spirit of life in Him has made us free from the law of sin and death. Christ, the captain of our salvation, has by His blood sanctified us and brought us to glory by His grace.

Ministerial Grace

"And the Word was made flesh, and dwelt among us, (and we beheld his glory, the glory as of the only begotten of the Father,) full of grace and truth…And of his fulness have all we received, and grace for grace. For the law was given by Moses, but grace and truth came by Jesus Christ." **John 1:14,16-17**

"But unto every one of us is given grace according to the measure of the gift of Christ." **Ephesians 4:7**

"But the manifestation of the Spirit is given to every man to profit withal." **1 Corinthians 12:7**

"By whom we have received grace and apostleship, for obedience to the faith among all nations, for his name:" **Romans 1:5**

"Who hath saved us, and called us with an holy calling, not according to our works, but according to his own purpose and grace, which was given us in Christ Jesus before the world began," **2 Timothy 1:9**

One of the outstanding effects of grace is our holy calling. The scripture declared in 2 Timothy 1:9: that we have been saved and called with a holy calling, not according to our work, but according to His own purpose and grace, which suggests every one of us saved by the blood of Christ has a holy calling, and all of our callings are as a result of God's grace. To this awesome truth, Ephesian 4:7

THE EFFECT

confirms that every one of us is given grace according to the measure of the gift of Christ. May I also add that the contest of this term is in connection with ministerial grace in regards to the fivefold ministry, namely: Apostles, Prophets, Evangelist, Pastors, and Teachers.

> *"For I say, through the grace given unto me, to every man that is among you, not to think of himself more highly than he ought to think; but to think soberly, according as God hath dealt to every man the measure of faith. For as we have many members in one body, and all members have not the same office: So we, being many, are one body in Christ, and every one members one of another. Having then gifts differing according to the grace that is given to us, whether prophecy, let us prophesy according to the proportion of faith; Or ministry, let us wait on our ministering: or he that teacheth, on teaching; Or he*

that exhorteth, on exhortation: he that giveth, let him do it with simplicity; he that ruleth, with diligence; he that sheweth mercy, with cheerfulness."
Romans 12:3-8

Romans 12:3-8, summarizes the ministries set in the body; the term grace here is used in connection with ministerial gifts, offices, and services. The point being that all ministerial gifts, offices, and services are a direct result of God's grace; therefore, it's by grace we are chosen and called into ministry. As Apostle Paul alluded in Romans 1:5: it is grace that qualifies us for our callings.

In 1 Corinthians 15:9-10, Paul unveils to us the wind beneath the wings of his success in ministry. He said: *"I am what I am by the grace of God"*; in other words, he became what he became only as a result of God's grace; he laboured abundantly by grace and accomplished all he had accomplished by grace. All ministries, therefore, are functions of God's grace and grace alone. Of Christ's fullness, we have all received grace upon grace.

> *"And with great power gave the apostles witness of the resurrection of the Lord Jesus: and great grace was upon them all."* **Acts 4:33**

> *"And the child grew, and waxed strong in spirit, filled with wisdom: and the grace of God was upon him."* **Luke 2:40**

It was by grace the Lord Jesus Christ successfully executed and accomplished His ministry here on earth, as a man anointed by the Holy Spirit. All the apostles functioned by grace to accomplished their destiny. You and I are not, and cannot be exempted from that same grace. Actually, there is no other means of ministry as far as the gospel of our Lord Jesus Christ is concern. Grace is the ministerial material for building God's house or doing God's work. Building with grace is building with gold, silver, and precious stones; while ministry apart from God's grace is building with wood, hails, and stubbles, which amounts to self and work of the flesh.

This parallel is the difference between Abel's and Cain's sacrifices. We would agree that though they were both sacrifices, one was of grace, while the other was of works. The sacrifice of grace was accepted, but the sacrifice of works was rejected. Likewise, will the ministry by grace be accepted and abide, while the ministry by works rejected and burnt up by fire? Dear brethren, let us be careful to do ministry only by the grace of God and no other means. Grace is the ability that God furnished us with for His service.

> *"As every man hath received the gift, even so minister the same one to another, as good stewards of the manifold grace of God. If any man speak, let him speak as the oracles of God; if any man minister, let him do it as of the ability which God giveth: that God in all things may be glorified*

THE EFFECT

through Jesus Christ, to whom be praise and dominion for ever and ever. Amen." **1 Peter 4:10-11**

"For we are labourers together with God: ye are God's husbandry, ye are God's building. According to the grace of God which is given unto me, as a wise masterbuilder, I have laid the foundation, and another buildeth thereon. But let every man take heed how he buildeth thereupon. For other foundation can no man lay than that is laid, which is Jesus Christ. Now if any man build upon this foundation gold, silver, precious stones, wood, hay, stubble; Every man's work shall be made manifest: for the day shall declare it, because it shall be revealed by fire; and the fire shall try every man's work of what sort it is. If any man's work abide which he hath built thereupon, he shall receive a reward. If

any man's work shall be burned, he shall suffer loss: but he himself shall be saved; yet so as by fire." **1 Corinthians 3:9-15**

CHAPTER FIVE
THE APPLICATION OF GRACE

"Let us therefore come boldly unto the throne of grace, that we may obtain mercy, and find grace to help in time of need." **Hebrews 4:16**

By *'application of grace'*, I mean the action of putting grace into operation or implementation. As the blood of Christ shed is not the blood applied, likewise, grace given is not grace applied. It is an eternal truth that the Lord Jesus died on the cross and shed His blood for all humanity. However, just because the Lord Jesus shed His blood on the cross for the sins of the whole world, it does not mean the whole world is saved; the reason being, the blood He shed must be appropriated. It must be received and applied; so it is with grace.

In the same vein, just because grace has appeared to all, it does not mean it is applied to all; it must be appropriated. To appropriate something is to take it for one's personal use. Although grace is available to all, it's only accessible by faith. Grace is God's power for solutions to all mankind's needs, but that power is only accessible by means of faith.

> *"By whom also we have access by faith into this grace wherein we stand, and rejoice in hope of the glory of God."*
> **Romans 5:2**

As implied in this scripture, the only access to grace is faith. Grace is like a required metal of vital necessity; while faith is like an exclusive magnet. As magnets are programmed or designed to magnetize metal objects, likewise, grace is programmed by God to respond exclusively to faith always. As pieces of metal naturally respond to magnets, so too does grace naturally respond to faith. Grace is God's provisional response to our needs, while faith is our reactive response to that provision. Grace is God's free gift to us through Christ, while faith is our humble hands that reach out to receive the free gifts through Jesus Christ our Lord.

> *"For by grace are ye saved through faith; and that not of yourselves: it is the gift of God: Not of works, lest any man should boast."* **Ephesians 2:8-9.**

The denotation of that scripture is that we are not saved by grace alone, nor are we saved by faith alone, but by both grace and faith. It was by God's grace that we have been saved, but it was also through our faith – even though our saving faith is also a gift from God. Hence, what differentiates the saved from the unsaved is not grace, but faith. God's grace has appeared unto all men, and it is readily available and accessible – but only those who humble themselves to receive it are saved.

In his book, 'The Balance Between Faith and Grace',

THE COST OF GRACE

Andrew Womack illustrated or likened grace and faith to salt. He explained that salt is a mixture of both sodium and chloride. Each of the elements are hazardous to health if swallowed in excess respectively. Sodium in itself could kill someone, while chloride in itself is also poisonous; but when mixed together, it is quite beneficial to our life.

The intended point here is that any of these two saving components – grace and faith – when they are each stressed above balance to the extreme, one elevated without the other, they are hazardous to our spiritual health and wellbeing. Most people overemphasize grace to the exclusion of faith and end up in the ditch of lasciviousness, while others emphasize faith to the exclusion of grace and end up in the ditch of legalism. Meanwhile, only those who emphasize both grace and faith as inseparable twins avoid the ditch of legalism and lasciviousness; and thereby maintain the balance of riding on the high and holy way of Salvation. Hence, we will do well to avoid both extreme ends of the spectrum and stay within the scripture. Grace is always a giver, while faith is always a receiver. Grace is God's divine effort to meet all of our needs, while faith is our heart's effort to receive what God through Christ has made available and accessible.

The Place of Faith in Righteousness by Grace

> *"Being justified freely by his grace through the redemption that is in Christ Jesus: Whom God hath set forth to be a propitiation through faith in his blood, to declare his righteousness for the remission of sins that are past, through the forbearance of God; To declare, I say, at this time his righteousness: that he might be just, and the justifier of him which believeth in Jesus. Where is boasting then? It is excluded. By what law? of works? Nay: but by the law of faith. Therefore we conclude that a man is justified by faith without the deeds of the law."*
> **Romans 3:24-28**

In making the case for our righteousness being a result of our faith in the grace of Christ, Paul argued in chapter three of Romans that: all of mankind are sinners in need of salvation. That the purpose and function of the Law was to give the knowledge of sin and make it exceedingly obvious as sinful, thereby convincing everyone of their guiltiness and stopping every mouth from boasting. He stated further that the righteousness of faith without the Law is now available for all as a free gift of grace, through the sacrificial death of Christ as our propitiation. This righteousness is conferred only on those who believe in Jesus and put their faith in His blood.

Apostle Paul concluded in verse twenty-eight of Romans chapter three: that we are justified by faith in the free grace of Christ without the observance of the law. In order to buttress his concluded point, in chapter four of Romans, he used Abraham as a case study and cited King David's prophetic testimonies. He made the obvious case that Abraham was not made righteous by observing the Law, but by faith; that because Abraham believed God, his faith was counted unto him for righteousness. He argued that to a labourer, their wages are not considered an act of grace, but to those who have not laboured but believe or trust in Christ's finished work, they receive righteousness as an act of grace. In verse sixteen of chapter four of Romans, Paul made a remarkable conclusion of his case study.

> *"Therefore it is of faith, that it might be by grace; to the end the promise might be sure to all the seed; not to that only which is of the law, but to that also which is of the faith of Abraham; who is the father of us all,"* **Romans 4:16**

This verse begins with the word 'therefore', which either implies a final conclusion or a verdict. In other words, this is the specific point he wanted to carry across to his audience. The essence of that lengthy explanation is to emphasis to you, the reader, one of the core concepts you need to grasp and take away from this chapter. Know for sure that inheriting all of God's promises is the outcome of faith and depends entirely on faith. God has designed it to be so, in order that the manifestations of His promises might be given as an act of grace – which make it stable and valid and guaranteed to all of His children.

This concept is what I refer to as *"the fairness of God"*; for the God of mercies, who is the Father of us all, in order to be fair and balanced to all His children without partiality, has in His infinite wisdom made exceeding provision for all mankind's external needs. All such divine provisions are located in His grace, but positioned only within the reach of faith.

To be sure that none of His children are left out of the necessary faith, Christ deposited in us all the measure of faith at the point of salvation, and also put within our disposal His written Word to grow our faith. In addition, He gave us His Spirit to help us and His servant to teach us. With all this in place, no one can accuse God of unfairness. We have no more grounds for a case against God, or to question why He would do for one and not do for the other. God's grace is equally available to all, but must be humbly received by faith on the part of all without exception. This is what makes God the just and the justifier of those who trust entirely in the Lord Jesus.

Grace as God's Rest

"And to whom sware he that they should not enter into his rest, but to them that believed not? So we see that they could not enter in because of unbelief." **Hebrews 3:18-19**

"Let us therefore fear, lest, a promise being left us of entering into his rest, any of you should seem to come short of it. For unto us was the gospel preached, as well as unto them: but the word preached did not profit them, not being mixed with faith in them that heard it. For we which have believed do enter into rest, as he said, As I have sworn in my wrath, if they shall enter into my rest: although the works were

finished from the foundation of the world. For he spake in a certain place of the seventh day on this wise, And God did rest the seventh day from all his works. And in this place again, If they shall enter into my rest. Seeing therefore it remaineth that some must enter therein, and they to whom it was first preached entered not in because of unbelief: Again, he limiteth a certain day, saying in David, To day, after so long a time; as it is said, To day if ye will hear his voice, harden not your hearts. For if Jesus had given them rest, then would he not afterward have spoken of another day. There remaineth therefore a rest to the people of God. For he that is entered into his rest, he also hath ceased from his own works, as God did from his. Let us labour therefore to enter into that rest, lest any man fall after the same example of unbelief. For the word of God is quick, and powerful, and sharper than any twoedged sword, piercing even to the dividing asunder of soul and spirit, and of the joints and marrow, and is a discerner of the thoughts and intents of the heart. Neither is there any creature that is not manifest in his sight: but all things are naked and opened unto the eyes of him with whom we have to do. Seeing then that we have a great high priest, that is passed into the heavens, Jesus the Son of God, let us hold fast our profession. For we have not an high priest which cannot be touched with the feeling of our infirmities; but was in all points tempted like as we are, yet without sin. Let us therefore come boldly unto the throne of grace, that we may obtain mercy, and find grace to help in time of need." **Hebrews 4:1-16**

Unlike the previous lesson, which was a case study

about father Abraham who received righteousness by faith as an act of God's grace, here in this passage of scripture, we see a case study of the children of Israel in the wilderness who failed to enter God's rest of grace because of unbelief. Thus, we are here warned not to harden our heart and fall after their example of unbelief. I submit to you therefore, 'that God's Grace is His rest that remains therefore to the people of God'. Only those who believe can enter in, but those who refuse to believe cannot enter into this rest. Notice that the works were finished from the foundation of the world. What work could that be? It's none other but the work of grace.

Every reference from the scripture regarding anything done before the foundation of the world is always pointing to Christ as a Lamb slain before the foundation of the world. That finished work is the work of grace carried into effect by the Father through our Lord and Saviour Jesus Christ. This grace of Christ that brings salvation is the rest made available to all men and can only be entered into by faith. Those who heard the gospel of grace preached and believed it shall enter into the rest of grace. Hence, we are admonished to labour to enter into that rest of grace.

To labour in this sense is to labour diligently in the word of God and prayer. Like the priest Ezra, we are to prepare our heart to seek God and His will, leave it and teach it (Ezra 7:10). Labouring also implies presenting all our members and faculties to God as a living sacrifice, refusing to be conformed to this age and, rather, choosing to be transformed into the image of Christ (see Romans 12:12).

Labouring in the Word includes studying to show ourselves approved unto God, a workman needed not to be ashamed but rightly dividing the word of God (2 Timothy 2:15).

> *"According to the glorious gospel of the blessed God, which was committed to my trust. And I thank Christ Jesus our Lord, who hath enabled me, for that he counted me faithful, putting me into the ministry; Who was before a*

blasphemer, and a persecutor, and injurious: but I obtained mercy, because I did it ignorantly in unbelief. And the grace of our Lord was exceeding abundant with faith and love which is in Christ Jesus. This is a faithful saying, and worthy of all acceptation, that Christ Jesus came into the world to save sinners; of whom I am chief. Howbeit for this cause I obtained mercy, that in me first Jesus Christ might shew forth all longsuffering, for a pattern to them which should hereafter believe on him to life everlasting."
1 Timothy 1:11-16

The diligent study of God's word and prayer is to build up our faith and make it strong to access grace. In Romans 10:17, we are told that faith comes, increases, or is developed by continuously hearing the Word of God. God's Word is the Word of faith, because it produces and engendered faith. God's Word is also referred to as the Word of His grace (Acts 20:32); this is because they are gracious words and activate God's grace to build up our faith for our inheritance in Christ.

Back to our case study, the writer of Hebrews sums up his case with an open invitation to all to come boldly to the throne of grace, so as to obtain mercy and grace to help in time of need. In order words, God's grace is available in His throne of grace, but you have to come by way of mercy to require, acquire, and appropriate it in your life through faith and humility. Grace is what helps us in times of need. In order words, grace is how God meets all our needs.

The Equation of Humility

> *"But he giveth more grace. Wherefore he saith, God resisteth the proud, but giveth grace unto the humble."* **James 4:6**

> *"Surely he scorneth the scorners: but he*

giveth grace unto the lowly." **Proverbs 3:34**

"Likewise, ye younger, submit yourselves unto the elder. Yea, all of you be subject one to another, and be clothed with humility: for God resisteth the proud, and giveth grace to the humble." **1 Peter 5:5**

Our gracious Father is the God of all grace, which simply means: He is the source and bestowal of all grace. As Psalms 84:11 declares, our Lord God, who is a Sun and a Shield, is the giver of grace and glory. Now that we know He is the giver of grace, but who does He give His grace to? Does He give His grace to everyone? Proverbs 3:34 seems to suggest otherwise, stating that God gives His grace to the lowly or the humble. Apostle James is very blunt about this subject, declaring boldly in James 4:6 that God gives increasing grace only to the humble and actually resists the proud. Apostle Peter, in verse six of chapter five of his first book, above, thus clarifies further that it is grace that exalts a man in God's kingdom. For anyone to be exalted by the God of all grace, they have to humble themselves under His mighty hand.

Why should it be so? Someone may be wondering: maybe it is because it requires great humility on the part of God to make grace available and accessible. Accordingly, He expects man to meet Him on the fair plane of humility – just as the Lord extremely humbled Himself to die for us a shameful death on the cross. It is fair that we come with the same attitude of gratitude in humility to receive the free salvation His grace has provided. It takes humility to receive the gospel. It takes humility for a man to say, 'I am a sinner in need of salvation. I cannot help myself; God, I need your help'. This is difficult for the proud to do and that is why God resists them.

The word 'resist' means to set oneself against; so, God sets Himself against the proud to defeat or withstand them. Hence, the Lord Jesus exclaimed to His bewildered disciples how hard it is for the rich, and high minded who trust in their riches, to enter the kingdom of God. Therefore, it takes humility to access God's amazing and abounding grace. Thus, humility is the acknowledgment of our inadequacy, undeserving, and the need for God to aid us throughout our lives. Indeed, we are not sufficient of ourselves to think anything of ourselves; our sufficiency is of God.

Grace The Trainer

> *"For the grace of God that bringeth salvation hath appeared to all men, Teaching us that, denying ungodliness and worldly lusts, we should live soberly, righteously, and godly, in this present world; Looking for that blessed hope, and the glorious appearing of the great God and our Saviour Jesus Christ; Who gave himself for us, that he might redeem us from all iniquity, and purify unto himself a peculiar people, zealous of good works."* **Titus 2:11-14**

According to the above verses, grace has not only

brought us salvation, but has also come to teach us. The Greek word translated to 'teaching' in this verse is 'paideuo', which primarily denotes 'to train children'; it also suggests the broad ideal of education. The connotation here is that grace is a trainer that has come to educate and train us in the way of salvation that we have received.

The scripture said to train up a child in the way that he or she should go, that when they grow, they will not depart from it. Likewise, grace has come to train us in the way that we should go, and as we grow in grace, we shall not depart from the way of grace. Hence, we must guard against any attempt of hell to remove us from the way of grace into legalism or 'liberalism', lest we be reprimanded as the Galatians were by Apostle Paul in Galatians 1:6:

> *"I marvel that ye are so soon removed from him that called you into the grace of Christ unto another gospel:"*

The essence of the training is to educate us not only to walk and grow in grace, but also to reign in grace.

THE COST OF GRACE

It takes grace to reign in life, so it is essential that we are educated in the knowledge of our Lord and Saviour Jesus Christ. This is what the ministry of teaching and preaching is meant to accomplish; it's not meant for entertainment, as it is now with some congregations, but for edification.

Someone once said: to train a child 'is to make them do'. So true! For grace to train us 'is to make us do'. Do what? One may ask. It is stated plainly in verse twelve: grace has come to train us to deny a list of things and admit new ones:

1. Deny Ungodliness.

2. Deny Worldly Lust.

3. To Live Soberly.

4. To Live Righteously.

5. To Live Godly in this present world.

6. To Patiently Await, and look for the realization of our blessed hope, which is the glorious return or appearing of our great God and Saviour Jesus Christ.

THE APPLICATION OF GRACE

The first thing grace is to train us to do is deny ungodliness. To deny is to abrogate, forsake, renounce, refuse, disavow, and reject. These are all strong and serious terms of denunciation, meant to highlight the severity of not heeding the admonition to deny ungodliness. Therefore, grace –if it is truly God's endowing grace – would train us to renounce, refuse, and reject ungodliness and worldly lust. Ungodliness here denotes impiety, which is opposite to godliness. It includes all that is contrary to God's nature and God's will. This proves clearly that grace is not a license to sin freely without consequences; rather, it's a license to be free from sin influences and dominations. As it is written in the Holy Scripture: *'...sin shall not have dominion over you, for you are not under the law but under grace'* (Romans 6:14).

Worldly lust, on the other hand, is basically desires for the evil things of this world. It could also be referred to as the 'lust of the flesh', which wars against the soul and resists it from doing God's will. All these and the like, which translate to the 'works of the flesh', we must abrogate, forsake, and disavow from our lives by the power of grace in us, if we are to live soberly, righteously, and godly in this present evil world.

Thus, grace is the power of Christ in us to live the Christian life soberly in this crooked and perverse generation. The Greek word translated as 'soberly' here is 'sophronos'; it suggests the exercise of that self-restraint that governs all passions and desires, enabling the believer to be conformed to the mind of Christ. In other words, grace trains and equips us with the ability to exercise self-restrain, enabling us to be conformed to the mind of Christ. Note that conformity to the mind of Christ equals conformity to the image of Christ.

Like the saying goes: *"To have what it takes, you have to know what it takes"*: to live a righteous life, it is essential that we are clear on what it takes. I submit that the same grace that it took for us to be made righteous is what it takes to live righteously. God did not make us righteous by grace that we might live unrighteously, nor did He make us godly by grace to live an ungodly lifestyle. A thousand times no. God made us righteous and godly freely by His grace, in order that we might live soberly, righteously, and godly for His glory in this present life – here and now.

Unlike the righteous, sinners sin, that's what they do. So, God does not expect them to live a righteous life, but He only expects them to come to the knowledge of the truth, to repent, and to receive salvation. Nonetheless, those of us who have received the abundance of grace and the gift of righteousness through Christ are expected to live righteously and reign in life. Herein is the saying of the Lord Jesus justified: 'to whom much is given, much is expected'. For this same reason, the scripture warns us not to receive the grace of God in vain or to no purpose (2 Corinthians 6:1). Grace not applied or utilized for the given purpose is grace received in vain.

Further Admonitions of Grace

We are admonished to exercise and abound in the application of the giving grace. 2 Corinthians 8:1-7.

We have been called into the grace of Christ and should, by grace, resist every attempt of men or spirits to remove us from the state of grace in which we stand. Galatians 1:6

We are charged to let our communication be wholesome and pure, so as to minister grace to the hearers. Ephesians 4:29.

Philippians 1:7 shows that a faithful and submissive saint is a partaker of the grace on his/her spiritual leader or mentor. 2 Timothy 2:1.

We are to know the grace of God in truth; in other words, saints must endeavour to become accurately and intimately acquainted with the grace of God in reality, deeply, clearly, and thoroughly. Colossians 1:6.

We are to fill our heart with grace and thereby worship with grace in our hearts to the Lord. Colossians 3:16.

THE APPLICATION OF GRACE

As children of God through Christ, we are commanded to let our speech be gracious, pleasant, and winsome at all times. Colossians 4:6.

We have been warned and so must be careful not to frustrate the grace of God. The grace of God can be frustrated when we set it aside to rely on our own mind and self-effort. To frustrate a thing is to resist or defeat its purpose. We must be careful not to set aside the grace of God, but rather to co-operate with it for our good. Galatians 2:21.

It is by grace and though grace that the name of our Lord Jesus Christ is glorified in us and it is by grace that we are glorified in Him. 2 Thessalonians 2:12.

In 1 Timothy 1:12-14, Apostle Paul credited his place in Christ and calling to God's grace that abounded exceedingly towards him. Likewise, whatever place we may occupy in Christ, one must never forget that it is God's grace that has given us such special privilege.

The grace for Saints to be made strong and strengthened inwardly can be found only in Christ

Jesus. So, take advantage of God's grace as your source of inward strengthening. 2 Timothy 2:1.

Saints through faith in the finished work of Christ have now been made heirs of the grace of life. 1 Peter 3:7. To be heirs of the grace of life means we have, as our inheritance, the grace of God that gives life and empowers us to reign as kings in this present life, and in the life to come.

Grace as a Keeper

"And thence sailed to Antioch, from whence they had been recommended to the grace of God for the work which they fulfilled." **Acts 14:26**

"And Paul chose Silas, and departed, being recommended by the brethren unto the grace of God." **Acts 15:40**

"And now, brethren, I commend you to God, and to the word of his grace, which is able to build you up, and to

give you an inheritance among all them which are sanctified." **Acts 20:32**

Both of these verses are referring to the same incident that took place in Acts Chapter 13:2-4. The scripture said that: while the leaders of the Church ministered to the Lord in fasting and prayer, the Holy Spirit gave them directives which they carried out. They fasted, prayed, and laid hands on Apostle Paul and Silas and sent them forth. Such faithful act of obedience to the instruction of Holy Spirit is what Luke, the author of the book of Acts, refers to as being recommended to the grace of God.

The word 'recommended' used here means to be delivered over to another to keep. It also means to entrust or transmit. Hence, they being recommended to the grace of God implies that they were delivered over to the grace of God for safe keeping; they were being entrusted into God's grace for their preservation. This simply proves that God's grace is a keeper or a preserver. Therefore, anyone entrusted into grace is kept and preserved by grace.

Further evidence in notable in Acts 20:32: there we also see Apostle Paul commending the Ephesians Church and her elders to God and the word of His grace. In this verse, Paul used a different Greek word for 'commend', which means to deposit for protection, to place alongside or beside. The point being that when Paul said, I commend you to God and to the word of His grace… he was emphatically saying, I deposit you to the charge of God and His grace for keeping and preservation. Grace, therefore, is a keeper and a preserver.

Grace for Acceptable Service

"Wherefore we receiving a kingdom which cannot be moved, let us have grace, whereby we may serve God acceptably with reverence and godly fear:" **Hebrew 12:28**

In the Lord's conversation with the doctor of the Law in Israel, Dr. Nicodemus in John chapter three: He said to Nicodemus, except if a man is born again, he cannot see the kingdom of God...; except if a man is born of the Spirit and of the water, he cannot enter the kingdom of God.

In order words, to see and enter the kingdom of God, one must be born again. To be born again is to be born of the Spirit and of the water. To be born of the Spirit is to believe in the Gospel and put your faith on the sacrificial death, burial, and resurrection of the Lord Jesus Christ; to acknowledge and confess Him as personal Lord and Saviour. This is what admits one into the family of God and makes one an heir of the kingdom of Heaven.

Unto those of us that are heirs of the Kingdom, the writer of Hebrews is admonishing us to have grace, whereby we may serve God acceptably with reverence and godly fear. The inference of the above verse is that: it is by grace alone that we are able to serve God in the way that is pleasing to Him. Like the old song says: it was grace that taught my heart to fear, and it was grace my fear released. It is God's grace freely bestowed upon us that enables us to walk in the fear of the Lord. And it is the same grace that frees us from the wrath of God to come. That is why it is an amazing grace!

Note: if God can be served acceptably, it also suggests that He can be served unacceptably. Unfortunately, there are so many, both in the circular and religious world, who presume they are serving God acceptably, but are not. This is why, as true believers, we must preach the pure gospel of the kingdom. There are just too many deceptions and delusions going on in our world today. Even the very elects are being deceived as the Lord forewarned. So saints, be warned! To be forewarned is to be forearmed.

Most Christians no longer have reverence for the house and things of God. They are unable to separate the precious from the vile, the holy from the unholy; this is a symptom of a lack of grace and of high sensual carnality. Anyone who may thus be desensitized by worldly and youthful lust should repent, humble themselves before God to receive grace to serve Him in Spirit and in truth – which is the reasonable and acceptable worship that God requires.

Establishing Grace

"Be not carried about with divers and strange doctrines. For it is a good thing that the heart be established with grace; not with meats, which have not profited them that have been occupied therein." **Hebrews 13:9**

The scripture is forewarning us here not to fall prey to those who seek to entangle and deceive saints with varied or strange teachings; the reason being that by such strange doctrines, the simpleminded are corrupted and lured away from the true gospel of grace and into utility gospel or legalism of the Law. The only antidote against such deception is to ensure that one's heart is established in the true grace of God. As Apostle Peter reassures and testifies to the saints, this is the true grace of God in which we stand (1Peter 5:12). Please, be sure you are standing in the true grace of God, and refuse to be removed into another like some of the Galatians folks were.

> *"I marvel that ye are so soon removed from him that called you into the grace of Christ unto another gospel: Which is not another; but there be some that trouble you, and would pervert the gospel of Christ. But though we, or an angel from heaven, preach any other gospel unto you than that which we have preached unto you, let him be accursed. As we said before, so say I now again, If any man preach any other gospel unto you than that ye have received, let him be accursed."* **Galatians 1:6-9.**

Growing in Grace

> *"But grow in grace, and in the*

knowledge of our Lord and Saviour Jesus Christ. To him be glory both now and for ever. Amen." **2Peter 3:18**

"Grace and peace be multiplied unto you through the knowledge of God, and of Jesus our Lord," **2 Peter 1:2**

"Now when the congregation was broken up, many of the Jews and religious proselytes followed Paul and Barnabas: who, speaking to them, persuaded them to continue in the grace of God." **Acts 13:43**

The instruction to grow in grace not only motivates us but also unveils to us the possibility of an ever increasing growth of grace. Our God is the God of all grace, which suggests that grace is varied. We grow from grace to more grace, to great grace, to greater grace, to an abundance of grace. The many benedictions of the New Testament writers say that grace can be multiplied and show grace is measurable and grow-able.

THE COST OF GRACE

To grow in grace therefore is to increase one's capacity to carry more grace. As holy vessels, to the degree our holy vessels are spiritually enlarged – to that degree, we are able to take hold of more grace. Our spiritual capacity is enlarged as we humble ourselves before the Lord. He only gives more grace to the humble (James 4:6). We also increase in grace as we grow in the knowledge of the Lord Jesus Christ. The more we humble ourselves before the Lord, the more of Him is revealed. To us, the more of Him we know, the more of His grace we receive.

> *"Likewise, ye younger, submit yourselves unto the elder. Yea, all of you be subject one to another, and be clothed with humility: for God resisteth the proud, and giveth grace to the humble. Humble yourselves therefore under the mighty hand of God, that he may exalt you in due time:"* **1 Peter 5:5-6**

The Word says as we humble ourselves under the mighty hand of God, He exalts us in due season.

How does God exalt us? God exalts a man by giving him more grace. It is God's grace that exalts a man. When God exalts a man, He honours and beautifies him with great grace.

> *"Surely he scorneth the scorners: but he giveth grace unto the lowly."*
> **Proverbs 3:34**

Fallen From Grace

> *"Christ is become of no effect unto you, whosoever of you are justified by the law; ye are fallen from grace."*
> **Galatians 5:4**

The background of this weighty phrase is that Apostle Paul, in his address to the Saints in Galatia, charged them to stand fast in the liberty they have received from Christ through faith in His grace. He warned them that to set aside faith in Christ and seek to be justified by the works of the Law (as Judaisers were persuading them to do) is to fall from grace. To fall from grace is to lose the effect and profit of

Christ. Note that the word 'fall' implies a height; to fall is to either drop from a high position or to stumble down. In either way, it is a downward motion; this signifies that grace is a height or a higher ground. Yes, according to Romans 5:2, grace is a higher ground wherein we stand. To stand in grace is to be in Christ, and to be in Christ is to be seated with Him in heavenly places.

Let's heed the warning and avoid any or everything that would attempt to make us fall from grace and lose the profit and effect of Christ. One other observation to consider in the above verse is that: it is possible to fall from grace. May that not be your or my portion. While it is possible to grow in grace, it is also possible to decrease in grace.

> *"What shall we say then? Shall we continue in sin, that grace may abound? God forbid. How shall we, that are dead to sin, live any longer therein?"*
> **Romans 6:1-2**

When grace is truly preached as Paul has clearly

THE APPLICATION OF GRACE

done here, this question is always on the air. Preachers that answer this question as Paul did usually bring a balance, but those who do not usually present an unbalanced message of grace. Obviously, as those saved by grace from sin, we should not expect to continue in sin and should expect grace to abound. No, banish the thought, it won't!

Apostle Paul used a stronger term to denounce the very thought of continuing in sin and expecting grace to abound. He said "God forbid"! That is as strong as it gets. Therefore, to continue in sin after one has been saved by grace is to decrease in manifested grace or, at the most, be stagnant in grace. One may argue: 'But the scripture said in Romans 5:20, where sin abound grace did much more abound'. Well, I am glad you are thinking smart by bringing that up, but let me assure you, that has nothing to do with one individual continuing in sin to have grace abound unto him. But rather, it's about abounding grace in the midst of tempting sin. It is grace abounding to a believer who lives in a gross sinful environment, as tempting sin abounds and the grace to overcome that temptation equally or super abound to the believer. It means no matter the trials or temptation or trouble that confronts a believer in Christ, there is a matching grace to overcome it all. This is what the Father meant in 2 Corinthians 12:9 when He said to Apostle Paul *"My grace is sufficient for thee…"* The same is true for all saints and servants of God in Christ Jesus; God's grace is sufficient for us all.

Fail of the Grace of God

"Follow peace with all men, and holiness, without which no man shall see the Lord: Looking diligently lest any man fail of the grace of God; lest any root of bitterness springing up trouble you, and thereby many be defiled; Lest there be any fornicator, or profane person, as Esau, who for one morsel of meat sold his birthright. For ye know how that afterward, when he

would have inherited the blessing, he was rejected: for he found no place of repentance, though he sought it carefully with tears." **Hebrew 12:14-17**

Not only is it a possibility to be stagnant in grace, it is also possible to fail of the grace of God. The Greek word translated as 'fail' here is 'hustereo', pronounced 'hoos-ter-eh-o'. It means to be inferior, to fall short, be deficient, lack, be behind, be destitute, want, suffer need, and be the worse. Simply put, to fail of the grace of God is to be deficient, destitute, lack, or be behind in grace; it includes falling short of the grace of God.

That is a state you and I cannot afford to be in; hence, the writer of the book of Hebrew warns us to avoid triggers of these pitfalls. Here listed as triggers are: root of bitterness, fornication, and profanity. These are what tripped Esau to fall from grace and lose his inheritance or birth-right.

Root of bitterness is a derivative of taken offence and unforgiveness. We must learn to forgive always, as we actually have no option on the matter. Unforgiveness is a direct disobedience to the command to follow peace or to endeavour to keep the unity of the Spirit in the bond of peace (Ephesians 4:3).

Fornication and being a profane person such as Esau is a direct violation of the command to follow holiness. The direct consequence of not obeying those commands is failure to see the Lord. Therefore, failure to see the Lord is due to deficiency of the grace of God. May the Lord grant us grace to follow peace and holiness, so that we may see the Lord's hand in all areas of our lives.

The COST of Grace paid by God through His Son is too high to take His grace for granted. We are to treasure God's grace and reverence Him who paid the high cost of it forever. Hallelujah!

CONCLUSION

On what better note can this precious book be rounded up than on the ageless hymn?

"Amazing grace!
How sweet the sound
that saved a wretch like us!
We once were lost but now we're found,
were blind but now we see.

It was grace that taught our hearts to fear
and grace our fears relieved;
how precious did that grace appear
the hour we first believed!

Through many dangers, toils and snares,
we have already come;
tis grace that brought us safe thus far
and grace will lead us home…"

Therein lays the potency of Grace. It rescued

humanity from the valley of sin's misery and positioned us in the hill top of right standing with God; with the unmerited privilege to reign as king in life. This amazing grace, though a free gift of God wasn't cheap. Hence, we are admonished by the scripture not to receive the grace of God in vain: do not take it for granted. It was so expensive that it cost heaven's best. If you were to ask the One who paid the ultimate price, He would sincerely admit to you, that it wasn't easy but it was worth it.

Sin made slave of men, but grace makes Kings and priests of men. Each one of us was like Onesimus, the run-away slave, who got saved under the ministry of Apostle Paul; and was sent back to his master not as a mere slave but as a brother beloved. Grace changed his status. In Apostle Paul's appeal to Philemon to accept Onesimus back as a brother in the Lord, he vouched to pay all his debt, by requesting that Onesimus dept be charged into his account. This is a mini picture of grace. As apostle Paul offered to pay the debt of a slave, so Christ paid all our debts of sin and ransomed us from the

CONCLUSION

slavery of sin. God charged our debt of sin to His account. Consequently, He that knew no sin was made sin for us that we might be made the righteousness of God in Him.

This beloved, is the high Cost of Grace motivated by the unconditional love of God. The guiltless and sinless Son of God became numbered with the transgressors; and for our sins was cut off. He died in our place, the Just for the unjust. This was the incalculatable price paid by God to set us free. Like Onesimus, we must return to God our Master and serve him acceptably with reverence and godly fear.

> *"And God is able to make all grace abound towards you; that ye, always having all sufficiency in all things, may abound to every good work"* **2 Corinthians 9:8**

May the grace of our Lord Jesus Christ be with your spirit, abound and overflow in all areas of your life, family and ministry in Jesus Gracious Name!

REFERENCES

1. The New Strong's Expanded Exhaustive Concordance of the Bible by James Strong. LLD., S.T.D copyright 2010 Thomas Nelson Publisher.

2. Living In The Balance of Grace and Faith by Andrew Wommack. Copyright 1997, 2002.